THE GREAT LIVES SERIES

Great Lives biographies shed an exciting new light on the many dynamic men and women whose actions, visions, and dedication to an ideal have influenced the course of history. Their ambitions, dreams, successes and failures, the controversies they faced and the obstacles they overcame are the true stories behind these distinguished world leaders, explorers, and great Americans.

Other biographies in the Great Lives Series

ACKNOWLEDGMENT

A special thanks to educators Dr. Frank Moretti, Ph.D., Associate Headmaster of the Dalton School in New York City; Dr. Paul Mattingly, Ph.D., Professor of History at New York University; and Barbara Smith, M. S., Assistant Superintendent of the Los Angeles Unified School District, for their contributions to the Great Lives Series.

GREAT LIVES

MIKHAIL GORBACHEV
THE SOVIET INNOVATOR

Steven Otfinoski

FAWCETT COLUMBINE
NEW YORK

For middle school readers

A Fawcett Columbine Book
Published by Ballantine Books

Copyright © 1989 by the Jeffrey Weiss Group, Inc.

Library of Congress Catalogue Card Number: 89-90816

ISBN: 0-449-90400-8

Cover design and illustration by Paul Davis

Manufactured in the United States of America

First Edition: September 1989

10 9 8 7 6 5 4 3 2 1

TABLE OF CONTENTS

1

The Man in the Street

GRANDFATHER IVAN IVANOVICH was the first one to see him. He was gazing out the family apartment window in Moscow from his favorite armchair when he saw the crowd of people. On this April day in 1985, he knew at once that something unusual was happening. After all, when does such a large crowd of people appear in the Proletarskii District of this great Russian city, unless they are workers coming from or going to one of the grimy neighborhood factories?

But these people did not look like ordinary workers, Ivan thought to himself. Most of them were well dressed in fur hats and dark, heavy coats. Some held television cameras and microphones. Ivan got up from his chair and crossed to the window for a better look. At the center of the crowd was one, lone man who walked briskly out in front of the others.

Who could he be, wondered Ivan Ivanovich. A visiting official of the Communist party? But what would bring someone from the government out here to their run-down neighborhood? Something terrible must have happened, he thought. Perhaps there had been an industrial accident at one of the factories. Perhaps this official was coming down to look at the damage.

In any case, this man who led the crowd could not be a very important person, Ivan finally decided. There was nothing important-looking about him. He was middle-aged, of medium height, stocky, and balding. Despite his neat clothes, the man looked more like a peasant from the country than a Moscow official. To top it off, he had a large strawberry birthmark on his forehead. It looked as if someone had dumped a can of red paint over his head. Yet why were these people making such a great fuss over him? Ivan decided it was not worth another moment of his time worrying about it. He returned to his comfortable chair and picked up his newspaper.

On the front page of the paper was a picture of Mikhail Gorbachev, the new leader of the Soviet Union. He was the general secretary of the Communist party. Ivan blinked his eyes and stared at the picture. This was the very same man as the one he had just seen outside in the street! They were one and the same! But, no, thought Ivan, it couldn't be possible!

Soviet leaders did not walk the streets like ordinary people. When they went to work, they rode in shiny, black limousines from their fancy apartments to their big offices in the Kremlin, the walled fortress which served as the government center in Moscow. The only glimpse common people ever had of them was on television or at big parades on national holidays. But here was their new Soviet leader strolling through the neighborhood shaking hands with people as if he were an ordinary person! It was hard to believe. Just then the front door opened and Ivan's son Nikolai came into the crowded, two-room apartment. There was a look of great excitement on his round face.

"Valentina! Father!" he cried. "Guess who I've just seen down in the street?"

"I know, I know," grumbled the old man impatiently. "I've just seen him myself."

"Who are you talking about?" asked Valentina, Nikolai's wife, coming out of the kitchen.

"The general secretary himself!" exclaimed Nikolai.

"What?" said Valentina. "You must be mistaken. What would the general secretary be doing here in Proletarskii? It doesn't make any sense."

"Maybe not," admitted her husband. "But he is here just the same. Come out and see for yourself. The whole neighborhood is in an uproar."

"Yes, yes," she replied. "And get Peter. He must come, too. This is a historic occasion!"

"Who are you talking about?" asked little Peter, coming out of the bedroom. His mother explained as she helped him into his coat.

Nikolai came into the living room, where his father was still trying to read the paper.

"Father," said Nikolai, "you must come with us. The general secretary is walking up the street!"

Old Ivan Ivanovich lowered his newspaper and glared at his son. "Are you deaf?" he replied crustily. "I told you I saw him. I have no desire to get any closer than that window. The police would probably arrest me. If you had any sense you'd keep your distance, too."

"But I can't see the harm," argued his son. "There's a crowd and lots of television people."

"Maybe we'll get to see ourselves on the evening news!" cried Peter, who was seven years old and had never seen anyone he knew on television before.

"Oh, go on then!" cried Ivan. "But leave me in peace. I've got better things to do than to run out into the street on such a cold morning!"

Nikolai shrugged his shoulders and left the apartment with his wife and son. Alone, Ivan tried to read his paper, but the noise outside made it impossible to concentrate. He threw it down in frustration and walked over to the window again. He was surprised to see the crowd had grown to three times what it had been only moments ago.

The neighborhood was alive with excitement such as Ivan had never seen before. People of all ages were standing in the street and talking excitedly to each other. Many were gathered in front of the neighborhood supermarket with their faces pressed up against the window. Could the general secretary really be inside? Surely the highest leader in the Soviet Union was not doing his grocery shopping in their dingy, little market.

4

Old Ivan's curiosity became stronger than any fear of getting arrested. He put on his shoes and looked for his coat and fur cap. As he dressed, he thought back over his life and the history he had lived through in his seventy-two years.

He was only a baby when the Russian Revolution took place in 1917. But he remembered vividly the stories his father had told him when he was a child about the czar, king of Russia, and his royal family. They all treated Russia as if it were their private playground. They ate well, hunted, and danced, while most Russian peasants and workers struggled to stay alive.

Finally, when the people had suffered enough, they revolted and drove the czar from his throne. They were led by a brilliant man named Lenin who established a new government based on the idea that ordinary workers would rule themselves, and share equally in Russia's resources. This way of life, called communism, turned the old Russia into the new Soviet Union. But then Lenin died. Ivan was old enough to remember that sad day, when Lenin's long funeral procession passed through the streets of Moscow.

The next leader of the Soviet Union was a very different kind of man. His name was Joseph Stalin and he came from peasant stock. He helped the Soviet Union drive out the Nazi invaders in the "Great Patriotic War" (World War II), but he used terror and fear to keep himself in power. Millions of people died as a result of Stalin's twenty-five-year rule, and the workers who were supposed to govern their own lives found Stalin to be more brutal than the czars.

Ivan had fonder memories of the Soviet leader after Stalin, Nikita Khrushchev. Also a peasant, he seemed to really care about the Russian people and their problems. He tried to reform the country and improve living conditions, but many of his reforms were unsuccessful. Other powerful men in the Kremlin grew nervous with Khrushchev's leadership. They finally forced him from power and sent him into retirement.

Leonid Brezhnev replaced Khrushchev as general secretary. He was cold and distant, like Stalin, but not nearly as cruel.

When Brezhnev finally died, more old men like him came to power, but they also died, one right after the other. The leaders of the Soviet Union seemed as tired and worn-out as their resigned people and the policies of their government. But, just in the last month, this new man, Mikhail Gorbachev, became general secretary. He was much younger than the others, it was true. But what difference would that make when things hadn't changed in the Soviet Union as far back as Ivan could remember?

Ivan Ivanovich had long ago lost all interest in politics. He, along with millions of other Russians, didn't see what difference it made who was in power in the Soviet Union. Life went on much the same as always, with its many hardships and simple pleasures.

The only man who had been able to inspire the people and really make a difference in their lives had been Lenin, and there were no more men like Lenin in the world. Ivan was sure of that.

6

So what was this Gorbachev up to? Ivan tucked his scarf around his neck, put on his coat, and opened the apartment door. He would find out.

When he got to the supermarket, there were even more people crowded around it, like bees around a hive. Nikolai and the rest of his family were somewhere in the crowd, but Ivan didn't try and find them.

"Is he still inside?" he asked a stout, sensible-looking woman.

"Oh yes," she replied. "The general secretary is still in the supermarket."

"What's he doing?" asked Ivan, no longer hiding his curiosity.

"He's talking to people," said the woman with amazement. "He's just walking right up to the customers and the clerks and talking to them and shaking their hands!"

Ivan shook his gray-haired head and tried to find a place at the crowded window to see for himself. But as he tried to push closer, the crowd began to murmur and fell back from the window. The door of the supermarket swung open and out came General Secretary Gorbachev and several other official-looking men.

As Gorbachev walked down the block, the large crowd quickly followed. He stopped in front of a factory and started talking to some workers. Ivan pushed his way through the crowd, far enough to hear the Soviet leader addressing a tall, thin man in his thirties who had large, rough hands.

"What's your job?" the general secretary asked.

"I'm a steam press operator," replied the surprised man in a deep voice.

"Do you like your work?" asked Gorbachev.

"Yes," the man quickly answered.

"And how are the working conditions in your factory?" The man hesitated for a moment before speaking. "All right," he said at last.

The general secretary looked into the man's eyes. Ivan was struck by the piercing intensity of Gorbachev's eyes. He seemed to miss nothing. "And what about your home life?" asked Gorbachev. "Are you happy with your living conditions?"

This time the pause was much longer. Ivan understood the inner agony the man felt. If he spoke the truth, the man could lose his job — or even worse, go to jail. To speak the truth had always been dangerous in the Soviet Union; Stalin had made sure of that. Why should it be different now? Yet, for once, someone had a chance to complain about the conditions that everyone in the neighborhood lived with. The crammed apartments, the dirty streets, the markets and stores that were always running out of food and other essential products. But how could an ordinary worker dare to speak of such things to the head of state?

"Everything is satisfactory," said the worker at last, his head lowered, as if he were ashamed of himself for being afraid to speak the truth.

The general secretary shook his head impatiently. "Is that really how you feel?" he demanded.

The man nodded silently.

"Everyone I talk to tells me he or she is satisfied with the way things are," said Gorbachev. "But surely there are some things that bother you, aren't there?"

He had turned away from the man and was now addressing the entire crowd.

"There must be some of you who have problems, things you would like to see changed," he said. "Won't you speak up? I'm listening."

No one said a word. Several people seemed on the verge of speaking, but thought better of it. Then all at once, a strange feeling came over Ivan Ivanovich. He couldn't explain it to himself, but something rose up from the depth of his heart. It was something that had been submerged for years and years. It was a part of himself that he thought had been dead for a long time. To his own astonishment, old Ivan heard his own voice loud and clear in the cold April air.

"I am not happy with many things," he said. Everyone in the crowd gasped and turned to him. He stopped, looked around, and then went on.

"There is not enough food and other goods at the stores here. The buildings we live and work in are old and falling apart. We need better homes and new factories. We need these things, comrade!"

Everybody looked with disbelief at Ivan Ivanovich, as if he had just dropped out of the sky. The old man spotted his family in the crowd. Nikolai was looking at him with his mouth wide open. Little Peter's eyes were as big as saucers.

The only person who did not look shocked by Ivan's words was Mikhail Gorbachev. His broad face broke into a wide grin. His eyes were shining. "Aha!"

he cried. "I can see you feel strongly about these things, comrade. That is good."

Ivan Ivanovich was too surprised to speak.

"Maybe, together, we can fix some of these problems you speak of," Gorbachev added. "I would like to help make things better. Does anyone else have a problem they want to tell me about?"

A dozen people in the crowd started talking all at once. Their fears had disappeared, at least for the moment. But Ivan Ivanovich heard nothing more that was said. He took a few steps and felt like a man who was sleepwalking.

Nikolai, Valentina, and Peter pushed through the crowd towards him. "Congratulations, Grandfather!" cried Peter. "You're going to be on television!"

Ivan mumbled something to his grandson and then looked back at Gorbachev. The general secretary was walking again, talking in a friendly voice to an old peasant woman who appeared to have a lot on her mind. He was waving his hands up and down as he answered her questions and encouraged her to continue talking.

"This is the Soviet Union," Ivan said to himself. "Such things do not happen here." Yet, people were publicly saying what they really felt, for the first time in years—right here in the streets of Moscow! This new leader, Mikhail Gorbachev, had started something, something that gave Ivan Ivanovich hope that he had long since given up on. There was something new in the air, and Ivan couldn't yet believe that he had lived long enough to see it.

2

A Peasant's Son

THE UNION OF Soviet Socialist Republics (USSR) is a vast land stretching across two continents—from the eastern part of Europe clear across to the northern part of Asia. It ends at the Bering Strait, a narrow waterway that separates it from Alaska in the United States of America. Also known as the Soviet Union, the USSR is more than twice the size of the United States. It covers more than one-seventh of the earth's total land area, over eight and a half million square miles.

Many people refer to the Soviet Union as "Russia," but actually Russia is just one of the fifteen republics that make up this gigantic country. Russia is the largest republic and the one that governs and controls the other fourteen. Russian is the official language of the entire Soviet Union. Some non-Russian republics, however, such as Georgia, Armenia, Estonia, and Lithuania have their own languages as the official ones within their own borders. Many languages are spoken by the more than two hundred and fifty different ethnic groups that live in the USSR.

Moscow, the capital, is a huge city with more than eight million people. Located in the north-central part of what is known as European Russia, Moscow is the sixth largest city in the world.

Eight hundred miles south of Moscow, just north of the mighty Caucasus Mountains, lies Gorbachev's hometown, Privolnoye. This humble farming village of 3,000 people is located in the Stavropol territory of the Russian republic.

Life here could not be more different from that in Moscow. Peasant farmers work the fields as their fathers and grandfathers did before them, growing grains and vegetables. It is a most unlikely place for a leader of this vast nation to be born.

Yet it was exactly here, in Privolnoye, more than a hundred miles from the territorial capital of Stavropol, that Mikhail Gorbachev was born on March 2, 1931. *Privolnoye* in Russian means "free" or "spacious." But freedom was something young Misha, as his parents called him, knew little of as a child. Two terrible events made Gorbachev's childhood anything but carefree.

The first was brought about by the Soviet government, the second, by the government's enemies. Gorbachev was born in the 1930s, when Joseph Stalin was the supreme ruler of the Soviet Union. Stalin had two goals—to be in absolute control, and to develop Russia into a modern nation. To achieve both ends,

Stalin set out to abolish the country's agricultural system.

For centuries, Russia had largely been a land of serfs, who worked grand estates belonging to the aristocracy, or nobility. Serfs were almost like slaves. They had very little freedom and were bound to the land they worked. Their lives were entirely in the hands of their aristocratic masters. In 1861, one of Russia's more enlightened czars abolished serfdom, and instituted a radical land reform. Former serfs became peasants and worked plots of land — some larger, some smaller — they now owned themselves. This new system of agriculture was far from perfect, but it produced enough food to feed the peasants, their families, and Russia's growing cities. Most importantly, it allowed the peasants a large measure of freedom from control.

There were still many poor peasants, however. One of Lenin's promises during the Russian Revolution in 1917 was that they would get more land. After Lenin died, Stalin was determined to change all that. He set about joining the small farms together into larger farms that would be run by the government. Peasant farmers, he said, would work more efficiently on these "collective" farms and produce enough food to feed the entire country. More importantly, Stalin would be able to control large farms much more easily than small ones. It sounded like a good idea, but there was one big problem. Many peasants didn't want to give up their small farms. They wanted to remain free and independent, however poor they might be. So Stalin used force to make them join

13

collective farms. The many farmers who resisted were deported — that is, forced out of their homes — imprisoned, or killed.

Forced collective farming led to disaster, not prosperity. Abandoned farms fell into ruin and famine spread across the countryside. Millions of peasants starved to death. What a world for a boy to grow up in!

But Mikhail Gorbachev's family was one of the lucky ones. His grandfather Andrei did not resist collectivization. Instead, he helped organize a large bread-producing collective farm the year Mikhail was born. Mikhail's father, Sergei, worked for the government machine tractor station, driving a combine, a machine that harvested grain. Both Andrei and Sergei Gorbachev were members of the Communist party, the only political party allowed to exist in the Soviet Union.

Although his immediate family was safe from harm, Mikhail surely knew friends and neighbors who had disappeared in the night, never to be heard from again. And, on top of collectivization, Stalin began an additional reign of terror in the mid-1930s. Suspicious by nature, Stalin believed that no one could be trusted. He began eliminating imagined enemies. Hundreds of thousands of innocent people — even loyal Communist party members — were arrested and killed on charges of treason against the state. Many more were sent to prison camps, known as gulags, in Siberia, a vast, frigid region in eastern Russia. No sooner had the horrors of these years faded than a new one appeared. This time the misfortune brought war.

In 1941, when Mikhail was eleven, Germany invaded the Soviet Union. Germany had been under a dictatorship since 1933, when Adolf Hitler, leader of the National Socialist party — whose members were commonly known as Nazis — came to power. A dictator like Stalin, Hitler soon exercised almost total control over the German people. Yet the ideology he imposed was not communist — which promised a worker's paradise — but fascist. Fascism maintained that there were superior and inferior races of people. Adolf Hitler believed that the German people, whose racial roots were Aryan, were vastly superior to any other group. He believed that it was the divine right of Germany's Aryan population to conquer and rule people Hitler considered inferior. Among them were Russians, who were Slavs; they were particularly despised by Hitler. Yet his prime targets were Europe's Jewish people, whom he vowed to wipe off the face of the earth. He very nearly had his way — over six million Jews died at Nazi hands during World War II.

Adolf Hitler also vowed to conquer all of Europe, a vow that led directly to World War II. Hitler had already invaded and conquered Poland, France, and many other European countries before marching on the Soviet Union.

The German army reached the Stavropol territory and occupied it for six months, but Privolnoye, being so small and remote, was not damaged by the invaders. Even so, the war years were still not easy for the Gorbachevs. Sergei Gorbachev, along with millions of other Soviet men up to the age of fifty, was drafted into the Soviet, or Red, Army. He served at the battlefront for four long years. Mikhail Gorbachev stayed home with his mother, Maria, and his sister, and worked the farm.

Mikhail had started his education at the age of eight, but the school closed because of the war. When it opened again, Gorbachev still could not return to it right away because he had no shoes. When his father, who was in the Army, heard about this, he wrote to his wife at once. He urged her to sell anything she could to buy shoes for their son. Even in the middle of a terrible war, Sergei Gorbachev knew the importance of a good education for his child. Mikhail Gorbachev got his shoes and returned to school. He repaid his father's concern by working hard at his studies. He was determined to make his parents proud of him, although he wasn't sure how he would do this. Especially since during wartime the whole world seemed so uncertain. Who knew what would happen?

Meanwhile, in 1943, the Red Army drove the Germans out of the Soviet Union. After two more years of fighting, World War II was over. Germany was beaten, and the Soviet Union, along with its allies, the United States and Great Britain, was victorious. It was, however, a bitter victory for the Soviet people. They had lost 20 million people in the war, more than anyone else. Their country was in a state of ruin, with entire towns and cities reduced to rubble.

Many years later Gorbachev would write about the destruction he saw while on a train ride to Moscow

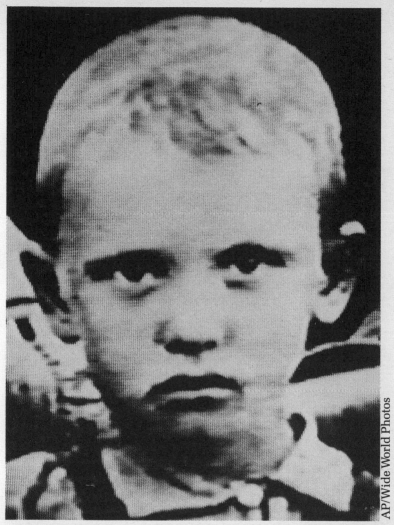

Mikhail "Misha" Gorbachev at the age of four. This 1935 family photograph was taken during the Stalin-era famine. It is estimated that many millions of Russian peasants died during this dark period of Soviet history.

soon after the war: "I saw with my own eyes the ruined Stalingrad . . . Leningrad. . . . Everything lay in ruins: hundreds and thousands of cities, towns and villages, factories and mills. Our most valuable monuments of culture were plundered or destroyed — picture galleries and palaces, libraries and cathedrals." These memories made a deep and lasting impression on Gorbachev. They stirred in him a deep hatred for war and a burning desire to see his country strong and proud.

With the war over, the job of rebuilding the Soviet Union began at once. Gorbachev, barely a teenager, now followed in his father's footsteps and operated a combine in the grain fields. He worked full-time during the summers and part-time after school the rest of the year.

It was not easy work for a young boy. Gorbachev was exposed to freezing cold in winter and terrible heat in summer. Soviet combines at that time had no cabs to protect the drivers. Chaff and dust from the harvested grain formed a cloud that engulfed him as he worked. He had to put up with these miserable conditions up to twelve hours a day sometimes.

Gorbachev worked as hard at his studies as he did in the fields. In 1949, at age eighteen, he was awarded the Red Banner of Labor. This distinguished award for national service was rarely given to a person so young. The following year he graduated second in his high school class and received a silver medal for excellence. By now, he was a member of the Komsomol, the Communist Youth League. The Komsomol was the only youth organization allowed in the Soviet Union. Similar to scouts in other countries, the Komsomol tried to teach the values of self-reliance and self-sacrifice to young people. But it also had another goal: to teach young people about the superiority of communism as a political system. Komsomol members attended meetings and lectures, published and spread party propaganda, and ran clubs and sports activities. Gorbachev was proud of his membership in the Komsomol and looked forward to the time when he would become a full member of the Communist party.

While every citizen of the Soviet Union can call him or herself a communist, only a select few—about six or seven out of every one hundred people—are actual members of the Communist party. A person applies for membership, and can be accepted on a trial, or candidate, basis. This candidacy lasts a year before the person is admitted to full party membership. Only party members are allowed to play an active role in government and only party members can hope to rise to the top in any particular field.

Young Gorbachev stood an excellent chance of becoming a party member because his father and grandfather were also party members. In 1950, he applied to the Party and became a candidate for membership.

About the same time, he also applied to get into college, or university. What chance did a peasant's son have of being accepted for a university education? In the case of Mikhail Gorbachev, it was a very good chance. His family stood well in the Communist party and he had the support of local Communist party officials. In addition, the universities liked to admit a certain number of young people from poor peasant backgrounds. It showed that they opened their doors to all Russians, regardless of their social status.

Still, when Gorbachev was accepted at Moscow State University, everyone in Privolnoye was surprised. Moscow State was the finest university in the entire Soviet Union. A graduate from there could become almost anything—a doctor, a professor, a government leader.

The question Gorbachev now faced was what subject to study. There were many schools within the university. Which one should he enter? What career, out of the many to choose from, should he pursue? It might seem natural for the son of a peasant to study agriculture. But those long hours riding the combine had taken away any enthusiasm Gorbachev might have had for farming. He was smart and he wanted to use his head, not his hands, to make a living. Gorbachev decided to enter law school.

Lawyers weren't highly respected in the Soviet Union at this time, and Mikhail's choice may have seemed an odd one. Perhaps growing up in the lawless years of Stalin's terror made him long for law and order. But it is more likely that he saw law as one way of getting into politics. Soviet politicians—all of them members of the Communist party—were the people who made a difference in the way things were done. In politics, young Gorbachev saw a way to fulfill his personal ambition to succeed and at the same time to help make his country a better place to live.

That fall, Mikhail Gorbachev left Privolnoye a peasant youth; bright, but basically uneducated and unsophisticated in the ways of the world. He would return home five years later with an education, a degree, a young wife, and a focus for all his ambition.

3

University Days

MIKHAIL GORBACHEV WON no popularity contest when he first arrived at Moscow State University. Students from more prosperous families frowned on his peasant manners and lack of sophistication. They laughed at his homespun clothes and country accent. But they failed to recognize that this young man from the provinces had something many of them lacked: a burning ambition to make a place for himself in the world.

Two people Gorbachev met at the university played a major role in shaping his life. The first was Zdenek Mlynar, his college roommate. Most students at Moscow University had Russian roommates with backgrounds and interests similar to their own. Mlynar was from Czechoslovakia, a central European country under Soviet domination. He was a cultured young man and an intellectual. Mlynar was perhaps the first true intellectual that Gorbachev came to know personally. Intellectuals—people who understand and value ideas—have always played an important role in European life. Drawing on philosophy, history, literature, and art, they often embodied the consciousness of a culture. To be an intellectual was as much a state of mind as it was a sign of learning and intelligence. The two very different young men became fast friends and went to films and plays together. Through Mlynar, Gorbachev became aware of a larger world beyond the borders of provincial Russia. For his part, Mlynar admired Gorbachev's honesty, loyalty, inquiring mind, and natural leadership abilities.

After graduating from Moscow University, Zdenek Mlynar returned to his homeland and, like his roommate, entered politics. But while Gorbachev remained relatively unknown in provincial posts through much of the 1950s and 1960s, Mlynar climbed to the top of his country's governing elite, becoming secretary of the Central Committee of the Czechoslovakian Communist party in Prague. He was a leader of a political reform movement in 1968, when Czechoslovakia tried to put another interpretation of communism into practice.

Until that point, the Czechs and the Slovaks had been forced to follow the Soviet Stalinist model of communism, imposed on them after World War II. In some ways, the 1968 reforms were a declaration of social and cultural independence from the Soviet Union.

The leader of Czechoslovakia, Alexander Dubcek, began to loosen the grip the Communist party had on

23

society, allowing more freedom of speech, and opening up the political process. He introduced the idea that non-party members could stand for office. Dubcek declared that he wanted to "give socialism a human face." This time of reform in Czechoslovakia came to be known as "Prague Spring," after the country's capital city.

The Czech reforms proved too much for the then Soviet leader, Leonid Brezhnev, to tolerate. Along with other Communist leaders in Poland and East Germany, Brezhnev was frightened that the reforms would spread beyond Czech borders, into other East bloc countries.

So Brezhnev ordered Soviet troops to invade Czechoslovakia in August 1968, and the liberal movement ended. Today, Zdenek Mlynar lives in the West, a defector from Communist-controlled Czechoslovakia. Ironically, less than twenty years later, Gorbachev would borrow many ideas for his own reforms from Prague Spring.

The second person who was to play a major role in Gorbachev's life was an attractive, intelligent philosophy student named Raisa Titorenko. Two years younger than he, she was born in Siberia, where her father was a railway worker. Later, her family moved to Stavropol, where she grew up. This gave the two young people a common background that helped draw them together. They met in a dancing class and learned they lived in the same dormitory, or hostel.

This hostel, called Stromynka, was hardly the kind of place to encourage romance. It was a grim, massive building built by the Russian ruler Peter the

Great in the 1700s. Originally a soldiers' barracks, in the 1950s, ten thousand students lived there. As many as eight students shared one room. There were no drawers or closets. All personal belongings were piled into suitcases and kept under each student's bed. The hostel had no bathtubs. Students trudged to a public bathhouse twice a month to bathe. About the only entertainment they could look forward to was American movies of the 1930s and 1940s captured during World War II from the Germans. The most popular movie hero was Tarzan, the Ape Man!

Despite the lack of privacy, the young couple managed to find time to spend alone. Gorbachev was attracted by Raisa Titorenko's beauty, bright mind, and energy. She was drawn to his sincerity, earnestness, intellect, and drive. They were married in his senior year in early 1954. It was a simple student wedding. Thirty of their fellow students joined them in a wedding party at the hostel. They spent their wedding night in his room, while his thoughtful roommate slept elsewhere.

It was a great relief to the young couple when they were able to move into a new thirty-four-story university building for married students several months later. They had only one small room to live in, but at least it was all their own.

Gorbachev worked hard at his studies. He was a good student, but not a brilliant one. He enjoyed math, history, and literature. He memorized poems that he can still recite by heart to this day.

But it was politics and the Communist party that excited him the most. He realized early on that his true love was not the law court but the political arena. Yet, there was one course at law school that Gorbachev loved: oratory, the art of public speaking. He learned the craft of speechmaking well. As his ability grew, so did his confidence, and he became a student leader. A former classmate later recalled how Gorbachev would make a speech at any and every occasion. He would lecture his classmates on the importance of the Communist party and the duty every Russian owed to it.

Yet, classmates' memories of him from this time differ greatly. Zdenek Mlynar remembered Gorbachev as having an inquiring and open mind, adding that Gorbachev often questioned the cruel tactics of Joseph Stalin, who had died in 1953. Other classmates, however, remember him as a hardliner who would scold those who did not follow strict party policy.

Regardless of which portrait of Gorbachev is more accurate, it was at this point that he began making a name for himself in law school. He also continued to be active in the Komsomol, becoming the group's secretary to the Law Faculty. As a Komsomol organizer, he worked in working-class neighborhoods of Moscow, handing out party propaganda and listening to citizens' complaints. He began to learn that the ability to listen carefully to people's problems and needs was as important to a good politician as the ability to speak well. In 1952, he was admitted as a full member of the Communist party.

Gorbachev learned another important lesson by studying the political life of his hero, Lenin. Lenin's ability to know when to retreat in the face of overwhelming opposition, and when to return to win another day, most impressed Gorbachev. This flexibility would prove to be an invaluable asset to him in the years ahead.

The ability to face setbacks was soon tested. Upon graduating from law school in June 1955, Gorbachev was not offered a place as a graduate student. Undaunted, he immediately looked for a state job as a professional Komsomol worker in Moscow. Here, too, he was disappointed, when an excellent job opening was filled by a fellow classmate. Gorbachev decided to return home to Stavropol with Raisa.

It must have been a disappointment for the ambitious young man to have to leave the excitement and opportunities of Moscow for the quiet, dull provincial life of his home territory. However, with his university degree, he could at least be assured of finding political work back home. He may also have felt obligated to the local Communist authorities who helped him win his scholarship and who, in part, had supported him in getting his education. He may have thought, too, that within a few years he would move up the party ladder and manage to return to Moscow, the center of power.

Yet, Gorbachev was to remain in Stavropol for the next twenty-three years. His climb to the top of the party hierarchy would be long, and at times, tedious. But when through a combination of hard work, luck, and political maneuvering he finally returned to Moscow, it was with more power than even he could have ever imagined.

4

Working for the Party

THE GORBACHEVS' FIRST years in the city of Stavropol, the territory's capital, were hardly memorable. With about 123,000 people and plenty of parks and trees it was a pleasant enough place, but after the excitement and grandeur of Moscow, it must have seemed dull and provincial to the young couple. Gorbachev's first job was as first secretary of the local Komsomol. His next job was deputy chief of propaganda in the territory or *krai*, as it is called in Russian. Here he helped educate young people in the "spirit of communism." He visited local Komsomol units and spoke at meetings in schools and factories. He helped supervise elections and attended weekly meetings of the Stavropol Party Committee.

It might have been a worthy position for a provincial person without an education. But for a university educated man like Gorbachev it was no prize. In fact, no one could recall when someone with his background and Party standing had ever taken so low a position in the territory. But Gorbachev didn't seem to mind at all. Like his great mentor, Lenin, he was content to learn everything he could, do the best job possible, and bide his time.

Home life held more promise and happiness. Raisa Gorbachev got a job as a schoolteacher, and in 1956, she gave birth to their first and only child, a daughter they named Irina.

Throughout the 1950s, Gorbachev was promoted higher within the Komsomol bureaucracy. Most of his promotions seemed to have less to do with his abilities and performance than with filling vacant posts. From deputy chief of propaganda he rose to second secretary of the territory Komsomol and finally to first secretary. He had risen about as far as he could in the organization and was ready for new challenges in the larger world of party politics.

In 1960 a man came to Stavropol who was to change Mikhail Gorbachev's life. His name was Fyodor Kulakov and, like Gorbachev, he seemed out of place in the sleepy capital of the territory. Kulakov had been an important person in the Soviet government and a close friend of General Secretary Nikita Khrushchev who was Soviet leader at that time. Khrushchev, a cunning and energetic politician, had won the internal power struggle within the Party for the leadership post following the death of Joseph Stalin in 1953. Kulakov's future seemed assured. But then he had a serious quarrel with Khrushchev, and as punishment he was sent to a provincial backwater

— Stavropol. As the new first secretary, his job was roughly equivalent to being a state governor of an area the size of South Carolina. Kulakov made the best of his "exile" and attacked the job of governing Stavropol's territory with characteristic enthusiasm.

He wasn't impressed, however, by most of the unimaginative provincial bureaucrats who worked under him. But Mikhail Gorbachev caught his eye. He noticed that Gorbachev was different from the others — soft-spoken but confident, business-like but full of warmth and charm. He was also an eager learner, who appreciated and looked up to Kulakov's leadership experience. Fyodor Kulakov was the first, but not the last, important Soviet official to recognize that Mikhail Gorbachev had potential.

He brought Gorbachev onto his political team, where he was made party organizer of one of the sixteen agricultural units within the territory. Gorbachev's last real experience with agriculture had been as a combine driver back in his home village and he seemed ill-equipped for the job. Yet he went to work with gusto.

Kulakov liked Gorbachev's spirit, so only nine months later appointed him head of all agricultural production in the territory. Gorbachev traveled all over the territory, making on-the-spot inspections of state and collective farms. Here Gorbachev saw first-hand how reforms and new ways of farming could increase production and improve the economy.

Meanwhile, by 1964, members of the Politburo, the fifteen-member top decision-making body in the Soviet government, had had enough of Nikita

These Soviet museum-goers are viewing a painting depicting Vladimir Ilyich Lenin addressing a workers' rally in May 1917. Lenin's call for the working classes to revolt against Russia's Tsarist rulers led to the founding of the Soviet Union. Lenin ruled the new Communist state until his death in 1924.

Khrushchev. On the national level, Khrushchev's land reforms, unlike Kukalov's in Stavropol, had failed miserably. Khrushchev was deposed and forced into early retirement. In October 1964, Leonid Brezhnev, a member of the Politburo, became the new Soviet leader. Kulakov's — and by extension, Gorbachev's — star rose. Kulakov was called back to Moscow. Within a year he was appointed agricultural secretary of the Party's leading policy-making organization, the Central Committee.

With Kulakov on the Central Committee, Gorbachev had a powerful friend in Moscow to help him in his career. But this didn't mean he worked any less as chief of the territory's agriculture department. He returned to school and studied farm economics at the Stavropol Agricultural Institute. In 1967 he graduated with a degree in farm production and conservation.

By this time, Gorbachev was also first secretary of the party Committee for the city of Stavropol. The following year he was appointed second secretary of the entire territory, in charge of agriculture. On April 11, 1970, Mikhail S. Gorbachev was named first secretary of the Party for the Stavropol territory. He now held Kulakov's old post. At age thirty-nine, Gorbachev was one of the youngest of the 181 provincial party chiefs in the Soviet Union.

He was finally in a position of real power and he grasped the opportunity. He restructured the territory's grain farms and expanded private plots for farmers, giving them an incentive to work harder. He improved living conditions by bringing electricity and natural gas into farm workers' homes and he allowed them a greater say over planning their farms.

His efforts gained notice in Moscow, and in 1971 he was made a member of the all-powerful Central Committee. As a new and relatively young member of this organization, however, he had little power or influence.

Meanwhile, Raisa Gorbachev was making her own way in the academic world. After Irina's birth, she went back to school and in 1967 received an advanced degree, equivalent to our doctoral degree, from the Lenin Institute in Moscow. Her doctoral paper was an in-depth study of the daily lives of collective farm workers in Stavropol. Her findings not only put her in the forefront of Soviet sociology, but also helped her husband to better understand the people he governed in his day-to-day job.

But then Mikhail Gorbachev was also his own unique sociologist. Every morning, he walked to work from his house down Stavropol's Dzerzhinsky Street. People stopped him in the street and told him their problems. He was a good listener and tried to help whenever he could.

A few examples show his responsiveness to the needs and feelings of ordinary people. Once, on a visit to a village in one district, a mother of six children complained to him that a manager of a state store had been rude to her. This was a very common complaint about store personnel in the Soviet Union. Soon after, the manager found himself out of a job. Another time, an application to finance a building for a circus in the city of Stavropol had been turned down. Party boss Gorbachev wasn't about to see his citizens deprived of one of their few and favorite forms of entertainment! He persuaded local organizations to donate the needed funds, and the circus found a home.

Gorbachev knew that the press was an important tool for his work. It kept him in the public eye and helped him get his message to the people. From his earliest days in Stavropol, Gorbachev made a point of regularly visiting the newspaper offices to chat with editors and reporters. And as first secretary, he held regular press conferences with reporters from all over the territory. He often challenged them to probe and explore more, and not settle for giving their readers the "party line" every time they wrote a new story. "Is anyone reading what you write?" he asked them.

Yet, outside his home region, few people had ever heard of Mikhail Gorbachev. For all his innovation, he was still just a minor provincial Party chief. And things might have stayed that way, were it not for the chronic health problems of a certain high-ranking member of the Politburo by the name of Yuri Andropov.

Andropov was one of the most influential men in the government of Leonid Brezhnev. He was the powerful head of the KGB, the dreaded Soviet secret police. Like Fyodor Kulakov, Andropov was a man of vision and new ideas. By the early 1970s, there were few men of this caliber left in the Soviet Union. Under Brezhnev, the country was beginning to stagnate. Corruption from the lowest to the highest level of government, was widespread. To get a good job, it was not *what* you knew, but *whom* you knew. Brezhnev himself bestowed soft jobs on relatives and friends, regardless of their qualifications.

Yuri Andropov looked on such behavior with great disapproval. He could see what corruption and decadence was doing to his countrymen. Many people in the Soviet Union just didn't seem to care about anything anymore. Life for them was barely worth living. Alcoholism was at an all-time high, divorce and suicide rates were up, and the life expectancy for Russian men was frighteningly low. Andropov knew that only by reforming the Soviet system and stamping out the corruption could things get better.

But Andropov was not well. He suffered from diabetes, complicated by a kidney ailment. To improve his health, Andropov and his wife visited a sanitarium every fall where they could take restorative mineral baths. The sanitarium was located in Kislovodsk, a district within Stavropol territory.

It was customary for the first secretary of the territory to greet important government leaders from Moscow at the airport or train station in person and then escort them to their destination. Gorbachev thus came to meet one of the most powerful men in the Soviet Union on a regular basis.

Yuri Andropov, for all his power, was rather shy. He had few real friends and didn't socialize easily. Yet he took an almost instant liking to Gorbachev. Gorbachev's cultivated manners and easy charm were a pleasant surprise to the KGB leader. Most of the provincial secretaries he had met were hard-drinking, basically uneducated men whose idea of a good time was limited to wild parties with plenty of carousing. That was the last thing on Andropov's mind.

Gorbachev was different. He was not only a gentleman — polite, and intelligent — but, most importantly, he was honest and incorruptible. He had an attractive and charming wife, who seemed to know as much about the politics and people in Stavropol as her husband. Andropov felt he had found a young man he could trust. Young Gorbachev became one of the few people Andropov could talk and relax with.

The Andropovs grew so fond of Raisa Gorbachev that they asked Gorbachev to include her in his visits to their cottage at the sanitarium. Mrs. Andropov found her good company on her long walks through the nearby park.

Each fall, the Gorbachevs looked forward to the Andropovs' visit. The two couples even started taking vacations together.

Then on July 17, 1978, Gorbachev lost his first mentor. Fyodor Kulakov died suddenly of heart failure. The agriculture secretary's death was a shock. Kulakov was the youngest and one of the most able members of the Politburo. If he had lived, he might have been the next leader of the Soviet Union.

At Kulakov's funeral four days later, Mikhail Gorbachev was one of the speakers. His speech was surprisingly different from the usual bland and impersonal rhetoric of Soviet leaders at official funerals. Gorbachev actually spoke of his dead friend with warmth and a sense of personal loss. His words were broadcast over television. Already, in their first glimpse at their future leader, Soviet television viewers got a sense that there was something different about this young man from Stravopol, something that set him apart from other Party officials.

In the following weeks, Brezhnev and his advisors set about choosing a replacement for Kulakov. It was not easy to find someone who could competently handle these important responsibilities. Yuri Andropov suggested Gorbachev for the job. He spoke persuasively to Brezhnev about Gorbachev's youth, energy, intelligence, and success with agriculture in his home region. But Brezhnev wasn't convinced. There were many better qualified men in Moscow who also wanted the post. They were older than Gorbachev, and had much more experience. There was also another consideration. Like Gorbachev, Kulakov had also come from Stavropol territory. Brezhnev didn't want to be accused of favoring this one region over all the others in the Soviet Union.

At Andropov's insistence, however, Brezhnev finally agreed to meet Gorbachev in person and then make up his mind. On a train trip to Baku, the capital of the Azerbaijan territory, Brezhnev made an unscheduled stop at the resort town of Mineralnye Vodi in Stavropol. He was accompanied by his close friend and aide Konstantin Chernenko. The two men got off their train at the small Mineralnye Vodi platform where they were met by Andropov and Gorbachev. During their brief meeting, Brezhnev was impressed by the personable, well-spoken Gorbachev. When Brezhnev's train pulled out of the station a short time later, there was no more hesitation. Within two months, Gorbachev was the new agriculture secretary of the entire Soviet Union. At age forty-seven, he suddenly went from being an unknown provincial party secretary to the twentieth most powerful man in the country.

The brief stopover in Mineralnye Vodi that day was significant for another reason that no one there could have known at the time. Three men, each of whom would become the supreme leader of the Soviet Union, and the fourth who already had reached that post, were alone together for the first and, perhaps, only time.

5

On to Moscow

THE GORBACHEVS RETURNED to the city of their youth with high expectations. Mikhail Gorbachev was about to enter the halls of power behind the walls of the mighty Kremlin. Raisa Gorbachev, who had been teaching Communist party history at the Stavropol Teachers' College, got a teaching position in the philosophy department of Moscow State University, her old alma mater. Their daughter, Irina, who was already studying medicine in Moscow, had just married a fellow student and was pregnant with her first child. She looked forward with eager anticipation to her parents' arrival.

Gorbachev knew from the start that his new job would not be easy. Success in agriculture had taken Fyodor Kulakov to heights of triumph, but failures in it had proved a political graveyard for many other ambitious politicians before him. Some of the Soviet

Union's agricultural problems were based on simple geography. Most of the Russian Republic is so far north that the climate is extremely cold and harsh. Leningrad, the second largest city, for example, is on the same latitude as Alaska. Only about ten percent of the Soviet Union's enormous land mass is suitable for growing crops and even this arable land is often plagued by drought and bad weather.

Partially for these reasons, the Soviet Union had been importing grain, meats, and other foodstuffs from other countries, such as the United States for years. Even with these large imports, many Soviet citizens did not get enough to eat. It was a problem, Gorbachev realized, that Soviet leaders had been trying to solve since the Russian Revolution in 1917.

Stalin's creation of collective farms that were owned by the state did much more harm than good. When he tried to carry this plan out, as we saw earlier, the farmers resisted and millions died as a result. The forced program of collective farms resulted in years of famine, misery, and a failed economy. Years later, Nikita Khrushchev tried to expand and increase farm production by bringing agriculture to the previously unfarmed areas of central Asia. But ultimately the plan failed and it led to Khrushchev's downfall.

As Gorbachev took office at the end of 1978, Soviet agriculture was doing surprisingly well. The country was experiencing the biggest grain harvest in its sixty-one year history. The 1979 harvest, however, was disappointing. Much of this was blamed on the lack of management before Gorbachev took over and he was not held personally responsible. In fact, Gorbachev was promoted, and his power increased so that he could work more effectively with lower-ranking officials throughout the country. He was also made a candidate or non-voting member of the all-powerful Politburo.

There was no improvement in 1980. Heavy rains flooded the growing fields across the Soviet Union, not only destroying crops, but washing away precious earth and causing serious soil erosion as well. Again, Gorbachev was not blamed for the poor harvest. Government leaders, led by his patron Andropov, felt he had done his best against impossible odds.

In October 1980 he was made a full member of the Politburo. By raising him to this highest circle of decision-makers in the country, it was felt he would be better able to effect real change in agriculture. Additionally, the other men in the Politburo — almost all of them a generation older than Gorbachev — needed the energy and enthusiasm of their younger colleague.

Mikhail Gorbachev at fifty-one was not only the youngest member of the Politburo, but a full twenty-one years younger than the average age of the other fourteen members. The "baby of the Politburo," as he was later described on a trip to Great Britain, watched the political situation developing around him with great interest. Leonid Brezhnev, in power now for over fifteen years, was in declining health.

Two factions formed around the increasingly infirm leader. One led by Konstantin Chernenko,

Brezhnev's closest ally and his handpicked successor, was made up of those men most loyal to Brezhnev. The other was made up of more independent-minded individuals. It was led by Gorbachev's mentor, Yuri Andropov, Foreign Minister Andrei Gromyko, and Marshall Ustinov, the minister of defense. As the battle lines for the power struggle were drawn, it became clear that one of two men would become general secretary after Brezhnev's death: Chernenko and Andropov.

Meanwhile, in the agricultural sphere, Gorbachev worked hard to turn around years of failure. He tirelessly supervised an ambitious farm program aimed at making the Soviet Union totally self-sufficient agriculturally in ten years. Gorbachev also made some innovations of his own. He transferred control over farming from bureaucrats in Moscow to regional officials. He established a "brigade system" whereby workers were assigned plots of land and given rewards as incentives for high yields.

But it was all to little avail. The 1981 harvest was the worst in six years. Only when the United States President Ronald Reagan lifted a grain embargo were the Soviets able to buy enough grain from abroad to make up for the poor harvest. (The embargo had been imposed in January 1980 by former United States President Jimmy Carter in response to the Soviet invasion of Afghanistan in December 1979.)

Newsweek magazine later called Gorbachev the "Teflon Commissar" for his uncanny ability to not only survive but also thrive politically, despite failures in the agricultural sphere. Like Teflon, responsibility for the failures didn't seem to stick to him personally. But the Teflon was now beginning to wear dangerously thin. Gorbachev knew that he had to show better results. His youth, energy, and friendship with Andropov were not enough to keep him in the Politburo if another harvest failed. Someone would have to shoulder the blame, and he was the most likely candidate.

The figures for the 1982 harvest were poor, yet not as terrible as those of the previous year. Mikhail Gorbachev nevertheless prepared for the ax to fall. It was autumn, and the annual celebration commemorating the Russian Revolution of 1917 was rapidly approaching. Each year this anniversary was celebrated in Moscow's Red Square with a huge parade and public demonstrations. Soviet leaders traditionally stood at Lenin's Mausoleum and watched as the parade passed by. November 7, 1982 the day of celebration, was bitterly cold. General Secretary Leonid Brezhnev was not well. But he stood for three long hours at the Mausoleum, as Soviet soldiers, marching bands, and tanks led the parade below. It must have been agony for him.

Three days later, Brezhnev awoke feeling worse than ever. He left his wife after breakfast to rest. When he didn't return after some time, Mrs. Brezhnev looked in on him. She found her husband sprawled across their bedroom floor, dead from a heart attack. The seventeen-year rule of Leonid Brezhnev had come to an end. A new leader would now emerge. Who that leader was, would decide the political fate of Mikhail Gorbachev.

6

The Second Secretary

THE POWER STRUGGLE between Konstantin Chernenko and Yuri Andropov immediately following Brezhnev's death was over almost before it began. Chernenko was not an impressive figure to his fellow Politburo members. A mediocre man, he had risen through the ranks mainly because of his loyalty to Brezhnev rather than any great natural abilities. Andropov, on the other hand, was a man of vast experience and had a proven record of achievement. He had been head of the KGB for fifteen years, longer than any other person who has held that office. He was quickly elected general secretary over his rival.

Andropov's victory was Gorbachev's salvation. Instead of being demoted from his post as agriculture secretary, Gorbachev now found himself assuming a much higher, although unofficial, position in addition to it. The sixty-eight-year old Andropov needed a right-hand man with energy and youth, who felt the same fervor for reforming the Soviet system that he did. The natural choice for the job of top aide was his old and trusted friend Mikhail Gorbachev.

Gorbachev's agricultural failures were buried with Brezhnev. The dead leader's ill-fated ten-year plan was blamed for being the cause of the recent farming problems in the Soviet Union.

Andropov had waited a long time for his chance to clean out the corruption and stagnation he had seen all around him. He wasted no time in getting down to work. Under his supervision, Gorbachev led a purge of party officials who were either corrupt or incompetent or both. One-fifth of all regional party secretaries were fired, along with thousands of lesser local Party officials and workers. Andropov and Gorbachev also "retired" many old and worn-out politicians and replaced them with younger, more vigorous men. They began to make the giant, sluggish Soviet bureaucracy more efficient and responsible to the people. They gave more power and authority to regional and local leaders. They introduced new Western technology into Soviet industry to stimulate the economy.

Andropov was anxious to close the gap between the government and the Soviet people. He hoped to renew public morale and make Russians care once again about their jobs, their future, and their country.

But the health problems that had plagued Andropov for years never went away. Within a few, short months of coming to power, Andropov's kidneys began to fail. He was forced to rely on kidney dialysis to stay alive. Soon, the once-energetic Andropov had difficulty walking across a room. He needed a younger deputy to carry out his programs, make speeches for him, and represent him in important government meetings. His choice, once again, was Mikhail Gorbachev.

As Andropov's aide, Gorbachev particularly enjoyed representing his country abroad. Ever since his university days, he had shown a keen curiosity and interest in other countries and cultures, particularly in Western nations. In 1966, as party secretary in Stavropol city, he went on his first trip abroad — to France. The purpose of the visit was government business, but accompanied by his wife, Gorbachev managed to take a side trip strictly for pleasure. In a rented Renault, the couple drove 3,400 miles through France and Italy.

In 1969, after the Soviet invasion which crushed the "Prague Spring" reform movement, Gorbachev led a Soviet delegation to Prague, Czechoslovakia. Official trips to other Communist countries, as well as to Belgium and Great Britain, followed.

Gorbachev's interest in other countries was unusual for a Soviet leader. Most high officials were suspicious of the West and took pride in the fact that they had never been out of the Communist world or even the Soviet Union itself. They reasoned that there was little they could possibly learn from decadent, capitalistic countries like the United States or Great Britain. Gorbachev knew better. The more he traveled, the more he saw that Western technology and Western societies were succeeding far beyond the Soviet Union economically. He came to realize that for his country to improve, it had to be open-minded and receptive to new ideas and ways of doing things, even if these came from the West.

In May, 1983, Gorbachev led a Soviet delegation to Canada in his first major trip abroad as a national spokesperson. The favorable impression he made on Canadians, and the media coverage that resulted from his visit, foreshadowed future visits to the West.

In Ottawa, the Canadian capital, Gorbachev met with the Canadian House of Commons and Senate and was asked some tough questions about his country and its policies. Brezhnev or Andropov would surely not have answered such questions or even put themselves in the vulnerable position of being asked them. But Gorbachev welcomed the often pointed questions. He responded to issues such as human rights violations in the Soviet Union and the controversial war in Afghanistan with disarming directness. He even admitted the Soviets made mistakes. This was unheard of. Soviet officials had a reputation for denying even the most blatant truths, and here was Gorbachev, being surprisingly open. When questioned about poor agricultural results he confessed the system he helped run was poorly organized, but also blamed the weather. "The only thing we really need, so to speak," he said with a smile, "is a little help from the skies." Both the Canadian press and public were impressed by his candidness.

After his visit in Ottawa, Gorbachev took a week's tour of Canada's farm regions. His host and traveling companion was Canada's agriculture minister, Eugene Whalen. Together they visited a meat-packing plant, a whiskey distillery, and other sites. Whalen was surprised and impressed by Gorbachev's openness and his unquenchable curiosity about people and how they worked and lived. Gorbachev confided in Whalen about his own country's failure to meet the economic standards of Canada and wondered openly why the Soviets couldn't do better. Everywhere he looked he got hints to the answer. Canadian workers were better paid and more contented than Soviet workers. The factories and farms had better, more efficient technology, and the system of free enterprise made for a more open, competitive and healthy, marketplace. Gorbachev remembered the things he saw when he returned home.

Back in Moscow, Andropov's health was rapidly deteriorating. He relied more and more on Gorbachev to be his spokesperson, attend important functions for him, and voice his concerns at weekly Politburo meetings.

Sharp-eyed observers of Kremlin politics wondered if Gorbachev wasn't being groomed to take over from his boss. But Andropov hoped that he would recover and be able to oversee the great reforms he had begun. It was not to be.

During the last five months of 1983, Andropov didn't appear in public once. He missed the Central Committee sessions held in the Kremlin and even the November ceremonies to commemorate the Russian Revolution. Never before had a Soviet leader missed these important events while in office.

On a chilly day in February 1984, Andropov's death from kidney failure was announced. Ironically, it was, in a sense, the very stagnation he had been fighting that killed him. A kidney transplant could have kept him alive for years, but the Soviet medical establishment lacked the technology to perform such a delicate operation.

Who would succeed Andropov as leader of the Soviet Union? Again, there were two serious contenders, and again, one of them was Konstantin Chernenko. The other was Mikhail Gorbachev. In the eyes of the other Politburo members, both men had strengths and weaknesses. Chernenko had strong ties with the Soviet past, a past other aging Politburo members shared with him. But Chernenko was also seventy-two years old and in poor health. Gorbachev was energetic, hardworking, well educated and had worked closely with Andropov. But he was still considered too young and inexperienced on the national level to take over the reins of power.

In the end, the Soviet kingmakers — that is, the other members of the Politburo — voted on the side of the safe and the known. They decided Konstantin Chernenko, a man with little education, no great experience as an administrator, and little knowledge of agriculture or industry, should be the next leader. Their decision said less about their confidence in Chernenko's abilities than their fear of turning over power to a young newcomer whose views often challenged the way things had been run up to now.

Gorbachev must have been keenly disappointed. He knew in his heart that he was better qualified than Chernenko to lead his country. He also knew that he had the resources to carry out Andropov's reforms

49

and the new ideas needed to fashion a new and greater Soviet Union. But Konstantin Chernenko was also not well. Once more, Gorbachev would be patient, do his best, and hope that his chance would come soon.

On Monday, February 13, the day before Andropov's funeral, a full assembly of the Central Committee met in the Kremlin, and Chernenko was officially elected to be the next general secretary. In a long speech, he vowed to carry out the reforms set in motion by Andropov. Gorbachev himself concluded the meeting with a brief speech supporting Chernenko. It was the first sign that he would continue to play a major role in national politics.

At Andropov's funeral, the next day, Chernenko cut a sorry figure before the national television cameras. The long meeting of the Central Committee had left him weak and tired. As millions of Russians watched aghast, Chernenko fumbled through a speech, running out of breath time and again in midsentence. When the military parade began, he barely had the strength to raise his hand in salute. Both Gorbachev and Chernenko were honorary pallbearers. Yet, Chernenko was so feeble that he couldn't even raise his arm to pretend to carry Andropov's coffin. Gorbachev and the other honorary pallbearers dropped their arms in a vain attempt to cover up their new leader's debilitated state. On his first day of power, Konstantin Chernenko seemed more ready to attend his own funeral than to rule a country desperate for energetic leadership.

At one point during the long funeral, Andropov's widow Tatyana started to cry. While the other Politburo members either watched stonily or ignored this embarrassing show of emotion, Gorbachev put his arm around the grieving widow and consoled her. His reaction showed not only his closeness to Andropov and his family, but also a human quality that would one day soon start to change the face of Soviet government.

Predictably, Chernenko made no great changes in his first months in office. There were no promotions into the Politburo and Gorbachev officially remained the secretary of agriculture. In fact, Gorbachev's position was as strong now as it had been under Yuri Andropov and extended far beyond the agricultural sphere. He helped the ailing Chernenko in any way he could. While the older man relied as much on Gorbachev as had his predecessor, Chernenko tried to show his own fitness by pushing himself to work harder. The end result, however, only hastened his own death.

As Chernenko's representative, Gorbachev was more visible than ever. Around the Kremlin, people were beginning to call him the "second secretary." It looked like the ailing leader was taking a back seat to his active and energetic lieutenant.

At the first session of the Supreme Soviet, Gorbachev was elected the chairman of the Foreign Affairs Commission. The office gave him little real power since the general secretary and the foreign minister basically set foreign policy. However, it did offer him more opportunity to travel abroad representing his government. On December 15, 1984, Gorbachev led a Soviet delegation on a week- long trip to Great Britain. The visit was a personal triumph for the "second secretary." His sharp intellect, warm humor, easy charm and eloquence captivated the British Parliament and public. On his arrival in London, he had a long talk with Prime Minister Margaret Thatcher. A staunch anti-Communist, Thatcher was nevertheless impressed by Gorbachev, and later told reporters, "I like Mr. Gorbachev. We can do business together."

Raisa Gorbachev, who, as usual, accompanied her husband, was as popular in Britain as he. Her chic clothes, attractive figure, and keen intelligence were celebrated in the British media. While the press dubbed him "leader in waiting," they called her "Soviet realism's answer to Princess Diana." Press photographers even bought her a bouquet of flowers when she left the country.

But the Gorbachevs' visit was cut short. The death of Marshal Ustinov, Soviet minister of defense, called them back home for Ustinov's funeral. This funeral was ominous for Konstantin Chernenko. Back in his office that summer after spending three weeks in the hospital, Chernenko had grown visibly weaker. It was a supreme effort for him to carry out public duties. At one event, for example, he read only the introduction to a speech and then handed out the rest of it in printed form to his astonished audience. On another occasion, Gorbachev actually had to prop him up to prevent him from falling over. Characteristically, Gorbachev performed this duty with grace, so as not to further humiliate a man who must have felt humiliated enough.

The year ended dismally, with the Soviet people once more disillusioned and all but leaderless. Chernenko rarely appeared in public. When his death was announced on March 10, 1985 after he had been in a coma for several days, it must have come as a relief to everyone. He was one of the last of the "Old Guard," those aging bureaucrats who, with the exception of Andropov, tried to hold together the pompous immovable Soviet state created by Joseph Stalin far back in the 1930s. After Stalin's reign of terror, they tried to keep the country stable and safe. They perpetuated a colorless, often corrupt society, with little incentive or hope for the individual. Now it was time for a new generation to take command. It was time for a change that, for many in the Soviet Union, was long overdue.

7

A New Kind of Leader

THE POLITBURO WASTED no time in choosing their next leader. An emergency meeting of the Central Committee was held the day following Chernenko's death. It took the assembled Party members only a few hours to vote on his replacement. Over the past several years and under two leaders, one man had proved himself ready for the enormous challenges ahead. He lacked long years of national experience, but, unlike so many older men in the Kremlin, he had his eye clearly on the future, not the past. Mikhail Gorbachev's moment had come at last.

Gorbachev's nominating speech was delivered by one of his firmest supporters among the "Old Guard," Foreign Minister Andrei Gromyko. "This man," Gromyko told the the Committee members, "has a nice smile, but he has iron teeth." After the toothless leadership of a string of old men, this was just what they wanted to hear.

Four hours after Chernenko's death was announced on Soviet television, the new general secretary, Mikhail Gorbachev, had already been chosen. His appointment was announced publicly the same day. The following day poor Chernenko's picture was pushed to page two of *Pravda,* the leading Soviet newspaper. Gorbachev was the page one story. The new generation was taking over, front and center. A new era was beginning.

If Yuri Andropov seemed to cause a whirlwind when he came to power, Gorbachev was a positive cyclone. In his acceptance speech he stated his top priorities in no uncertain terms — to get the Soviet economy moving and growing and to develop democracy and "socialist self-government." To appease the majority of conservatives in the Kremlin, at the same time he vowed to maintain a strong defense to keep a "peaceful coexistence" with the West.

Gorbachev realized he had to move slowly and carefully at first. Until he had consolidated his power, he was at the mercy of the "Old Guard" who still had a strong grip on the government, even if they had chosen him their leader. He set about loosening that grip by replacing hard-line Party members with those sympathetic to change and reform. Within a month of his election, he appointed three of Andropov's followers to the Politburo, and later added two of his own men. He now had a secure majority in this ruling decision-making body to get his policies pushed through. Within his first year as leader of the

Soviet Union, Gorbachev appointed thirty out of eighty national ministers and replaced about 40 percent of the Central Committee.

He followed Andropov's lead and removed corrupt and lazy party officials wherever he found them. The new men who replaced them were, for the most part, young, ambitious, hardworking, and as progressive as the man who hired them.

The drive to shake up the economy took on many forms. Cash bonuses and hard-to-get consumer goods were used as incentives to encourage workers to work harder and more effectively. Managers in industry and agriculture were given more power and independence to boost sagging productivity. New technology such as computer products, previously all but unknown in the Soviet Union, were brought in to make work easier and more efficient.

To get his message across, Gorbachev took a bold step, unprecedented in Soviet history since Lenin. He went directly to the people. His famous "walkabout" in Proletarskii District, where Ivan and his family saw him, was just the first of many such visits to neighborhoods in Moscow and elsewhere in the Soviet Union. Everywhere Gorbachev went he shook hands and chatted with workers in factories and hospitals, shoppers in supermarkets and stores, students and teachers in schools, and even over a cup of tea with young couples in their modest apartments. Like his great counterpart in the West, United States President Ronald Reagan, Gorbachev saw himself as a "great communicator" who could win the hearts and minds of his people by talking and listening to them.

At first, people were wary about speaking their minds. During Stalin's time, speaking your mind could cost you your life. In Brezhnev's regime, it could mean a jail sentence in a prison camp in Siberia. Now suddenly, here was a leader who told people they had nothing to fear for being honest and frank.

They soon began to be just that. A chief surgeon complained to the new general secretary that his hospital was understaffed and poorly supplied, lacking necessary equipment and medicine. He said that he and his colleagues earned less to perform an operation than a taxi driver did for a single good fare. Gorbachev listened and took action. At a Politburo meeting soon after, doctors were given a slight raise in salary. It was not enough to correct the problem, but a short time before even this measure would have been unthinkable.

A master at public relations, Gorbachev got back much more than he gave. The Soviet media, given unheard of access to the their leader, made him a superstar both at home and abroad. Foreign leaders around the world were impressed. Western journalists called him "bright," of "high intelligence," and "incisive." Newspapers and magazines were flooded with his picture and his words. He was a hit on television.

Gorbachev's private lifestyle was as appealing as his public one. Although he was driven to work in a ZIL, the Russian equivalent to a Rolls-Royce, no train of limousines accompanied him. When he lunched outside his office it was often alone at a local restaurant, where he was treated just like any other paying customer. Even at the theater, one of his great loves, the new general secretary refused special privileges. He sat in regular seats with his wife Raisa Gorbachev instead of in the special government box. Not that there was much time for fun; Gorbachev often didn't leave the Kremlin until ten o'clock at night. This prompted his granddaughter Oksana to complain "You work too hard, Grandpa. I never see you."

Confident he had the public's full attention, Gorbachev decided the time was right to embark on his first major reform. His targeted foe was not corrupt officials or Western capitalists, but a much more elusive enemy — alcohol.

Vodka is the national drink of Russia. Under the Soviet government, Gorbachev realized that vodka was the "opiate of the masses," an accusation that Karl Marx, the atheist father of Communism, had leveled at religion over one hundred years earlier. It was not surprising why vodka was now such an opiate. Life in the Soviet Union was often hard and boring for many people. Crowded apartments provided little privacy, there was much frustration and few diversions other than alcohol. There were an estimated nine million alcoholics in the Soviet Union. Nearly half of the work force admitted to drinking before work or on the job. The cost to the country's economy was about $8 billion annually in lost production. Alcoholism also contributed to increased crime, family strife, car accidents, poor health, and shorter life expectancy. Gorbachev was determined to put an end to this economic and human waste.

In May 1985, he passed new laws that raised the minimum drinking age from eighteen to twenty-one, prohibited the selling of alcohol before two o'clock in the afternoon, and restricted restaurants from serving more than two drinks with a meal. People who were found drunk in public or at the workplace were charged heavy fines or imprisoned. Gorbachev's crusade extended to the political hierarchy as well. Alcohol was banned from embassy parties and other official functions. Previously hard-drinking commissars suddenly found themselves toasting each other with fruit juice.

Many Russians applauded Gorbachev's efforts, but many more came to resent them. The long lines of people waiting outside liquor stores became known as "Gorbachev's nooses." Heavy drinkers who couldn't get their daily quota of vodka started drinking cologne for its alcoholic content. As a result, many stores stopped selling the otherwise harmless liquid. Other more enterprising drinkers made their own brew in illegal stills, risking arrest. Still others turned to the black market to quench their thirst.

Gorbachev was forced to admit that his anti-vodka campaign was less than a booming success. It was, however, also not a total defeat. Consumption of vodka was down and worker productivity was up. Moreover, he had learned an important lesson. Morality cannot be legislated and human nature cannot be changed by passing a law. People have to be persuaded to do the right thing. In the future, he would remember this lesson as he dealt with other problems both at home and abroad.

Gorbachev proved his flexibility by easing up on the new laws against alcohol and turning his attention to other issues.

In the summer of 1985, Gorbachev traveled extensively around the Soviet Union. He took his message of reform to every corner of his vast domain. He visited the Ukraine, then Byelorussia, and the Tyumen region, containing the richest oil fields in the Soviet Union. Everywhere he went he asked people what was on their minds. He enjoyed a good argument and was always ready with a sharp observation. He proved, with the instinct of a master politician, that he had the "common touch."

The ceremony and pomp with which previous Soviet leaders had surrounded themselves was not for him. At a meeting, for example, he would not sit on a chair, if sitting on a table brought him closer to the audience. It had been a Soviet tradition for young girls to present large bouquets of flowers to visiting Russian leaders. Gorbachev refused the flowers, telling the surprised girls to keep them for themselves.

When he delivered a speech it was often without a prepared text. The words seemed to flow naturally from him, like a river. He spoke eloquently, but also simply, using language the common people of the region he was visiting could understand. One Moscow citizen put it well when he said, "He talks normally, even pronouncing words like an ordinary mortal."

But like other "ordinary mortals," Mikhail Gorbachev was not perfect. For all his talk about change and growth there had been little of either during his first nine months in power. Conservatives distrusted him, and intellectuals, who were at first encouraged, were growing quickly disillusioned. He had changed the face of the Politburo and the Central Committee to reflect his own policies, but he had done little of substance with his new-found authority. The anti-drinking campaign had been a mistake (although not a total one) and he seemed reluctant to take on another big issue. Gorbachev was quick to criticize his own government's inadequacies but appeared to have no clear solutions himself. He had done little yet in the area of human rights violations and was wary of getting too friendly with the United States, for fear of losing support from the Party's staunch conservative wing.

He was like a man on a wagon who whips his horses into a frenzy, and then when they're off and running, doesn't know in which direction to go. As 1985 ended and a new year began, Mikhail Gorbachev knew he would have to back up his strong words with concrete action. The country and the world were waiting to see what this new kind of Soviet leader would do next. He would not disappoint them.

8

Winds of Change

IN FEBRUARY 1986, after eleven months in office, Mikhail Gorbachev opened the 27th Soviet Communist Party Congress with a keynote speech that lasted five and a half hours. Although he said many significant things, the most important just might have been a single cough. It came late in the speech and quickly developed from one cough into an outright fit. When he finally regained control, Gorbachev looked out at the sea of faces in the massive Palace of Congresses and said with a wry smile, "I am coming to the end." Tenseness left the faces of the 5,000 delegates. Someone actually laughed. The laughter quickly spread until it was a tidal wave flooding the huge, somber hall. That a Soviet leader could make gentle fun of himself during such a serious occasion was astonishing in itself. But that the assembled party members could join in on the joke would have been unthinkable at any of the previous twenty-six congresses. There was change in the air, and everyone could feel its power.

In his keynote speech, Gorbachev made it clear that he was breaking with the past — not the past of Lenin and his Communist revolution, but the repressive and stultifying past of Soviet leaders from Stalin to Brezhnev. "We have to part ways with those who hope that everything will settle down and return to the old lines," he told the delegates. "That will not happen, comrades."

While he pledged to continue his systematic removal of those who "discredit the name of Communist," he also outlined new programs to develop the country's sagging economy. A top priority, not surprisingly, was agriculture. To be able to feed its millions of people, he said, the Soviet Union had to have better technology to increase harvests and give more independence to those who managed state farms.

But Gorbachev also lashed out against the United States, whose imperialistic militarism, he claimed, was the world's greatest threat to future peace. The message was a mixed one — part progressive and part reactionary. It reflected the two main forces that Gorbachev had to keep in balance — the new generation he had brought into the government that wanted change and the older, more conservative politicians he could not afford to have turn against him.

But regardless of which side they were on, every delegate walked away from this historic congress with a firm conviction that here at last was a national leader who would lead them forward with force and conviction.

Not content with speeches, Gorbachev also wrote a book about his goals for the Soviet Union. He called it *Perestroika — New Thinking for Our Country and the World. Perestroika* is the Russian word for "restructuring" and that's exactly what Gorbachev felt was needed to make the Soviet Union a major world power economically and socially. As the title suggested, Gorbachev believed all countries could benefit from this new way of thinking. " . . . the whole world needs restructuring . . . a fundamental change," he wrote. "We are all passengers aboard one ship, the Earth, and we must not allow it to be wrecked. There will be no second Noah's Ark."

The goal of perestroika in his own country, he insisted, was no less than a "a thorough renewal of every aspect of Soviet life — economic, social, political and moral." Perestroika would unite socialism with democracy and together they would spell "more dignity and self-respect for the individual."

In order for perestroika to be successful, however, there also had to be more openness, or *glasnost,* another Russian word. Gorbachev claimed glasnost was at work in the 27th Party Congress where "we spoke openly about the shortcomings, errors, and difficulties." He had made glasnost part of his leadership style in his relationships with others, and now he wanted to extend it throughout Soviet society. "We need no dark corners where mold can reappear," he wrote. " . . . That's why there must be more light." Back in April 1985, Grandfather Ivan had experienced glasnost firsthand in Proletarskii.

Perhaps the most remarkable aspect of Gorbachev's book was that it was written not for his own people but for a Western audience, particularly the people of the United States. When first published in English translation in 1987, it caused quite a stir. Western reviewers found the writing style somewhat bland, but the message bold and exciting. The new Soviet leader was questioning his own form of government and challenging other nations to also change in order to meet the needs of the modern world. "In the course of the restructuring," Gorbachev wrote in his conclusion, "we are expanding and clarifying our notions about the yesterday, today, and tomorrow of socialism. We are discovering ourselves anew."

The words sounded fine, but would actions back them up? How does, for example, one man go about reforming a system that has seen little or no change in seventy years? How does he go about opening up windows in a stuffy house of state that have remained firmly shut for generations?

Gorbachev was quick to admit that perestroika would take time, perhaps a decade. But glasnost, the new openness, could be put in practice more quickly. And it was. Gorbachev saw glasnost as not simply an end in itself, but a way of creating a positive atmosphere in society that would help both the government and its people to face up to real problems and find new ways to solve them. The results were not exactly the kind of freedoms we enjoy in the United States, for glasnost did not mean a total freedom of speech. Gorbachev himself, for example, could not be criticized in public, in newspapers or on television, like Western leaders often are. But the changes in what could now be spoken about in the open were nevertheless earthshaking for the Soviet people. For the first time in memory, newspapers and television were allowed to do true investigative reporting, delving into problems that had previously been taboo. Misleading social and economic statistics were replaced in the press by accurate figures, no matter how unflattering. Soviet television even broadcast a probing documentary from the United States about Soviet emigres there, who had previously been considered little better than traitors for leaving the USSR. In the broadcast they were openly critical of the Soviet system.

Previously banned authors were published in the Soviet Union for the first time. Soviet citizens were now allowed to read important books like *The Children of Arbat* by Anatoly Rybakov and *Doctor Zhivago* by Boris Pasternak. There was less censorship — although it was not done away with altogether — and more creative freedom allowed writers, filmmakers, and other artists. Even rock music, once considered decadent noise from the West, was given official approval. Formerly underground Soviet rock bands suddenly found themselves performing at government-sponsored rock festivals.

News briefings for the foreign press became a regular occurrence at the Foreign Ministry. Western journalists were allowed to talk directly with government officials and even occasionally inspect sensitive

The Bettmann Archive

Vladimir Ilyich Lenin (left), leader of the Russian revolution,
seated with his successor as Communist Party chief, Joseph Stalin.
It is another Soviet leader—Nikita Khrushchev—whom
Gorbachev most resembles in his efforts to transform Soviet
society. With his program of perestroika (Russian for
"restructuring"), Gorbachev is hoping to succeed where
Khrushchev failed.

military installations which had once been strictly forbidden to foreigners.

The new openness, however, did have its "dark corners." While private individuals were fair game for public criticism, no one except the general secretary himself could speak out against the Soviet military, the KGB, or high-ranking officials. Gorbachev was bold enough to openly condemn and remove from office Moscow's number-one criminal investigator for drunkenness, and the party head of the central Asian republic of Kazakhstan for corruption.

Glasnost faced what may have been its biggest challenge on April 25, 1986. That day, an explosion blew off the top of a nuclear reactor at a nuclear power plant at Chernobyl, just eighty miles north of the Soviet Union's third largest city, Kiev, in the Ukraine. Thirty-one people died as a direct result of the explosion and the fire that followed it, while another six thousand people in the area were expected to die in the future from cancer caused by the radioactive fallout. The radioactivity spread out from the Soviet Union in an ominous cloud over nearby countries such as Sweden, Finland, Poland, and West Germany, devastating the environment and killing plant and animal life.

Faced by the worst civilian nuclear disaster ever, Soviet officials at first retreated to the old Soviet policy of secrecy. A full forty-eight hours passed before the world learned of the Chernobyl accident. Except for a silent appearance at the national May Day Parade in Red Square, where he kept his face covered from the cameras behind a black hat, Gorbachev disappeared from public view for nearly three weeks. By distancing himself from the disaster, which he blamed on his predecessors, Gorbachev tried to avoid serious personal criticism.

When he finally appeared on national television, it was to announce that the most immediate danger was over and that it was time to assess the damage and bring those responsible to account. Here, his actions were swift and decisive. The officials in charge of nuclear power on a national level were dismissed for neglecting safety issues. In an unprecedented move, foreign experts on radiation and nuclear power were asked to come to the Soviet Union and lend their assistance. A lengthy report detailing the disaster and its causes was published. The report was praised internationally for its thoroughness and honesty in admitting human errors that were responsible for the nuclear accident.

Finally, based on recommendations by foreign experts, Gorbachev passed stricter laws to try to prevent such a tragedy from happening again in the Soviet Union. If it is possible to come out of such a tragedy looking like a winner, Gorbachev managed to do it.

Another sensitive area was that of human rights. For decades, those individuals who spoke their own minds, whether against the Soviet system, or simply in conflict with the official version of things, were thrown into prison or exiled to far-off regions, such as harsh Siberia. Minority groups, especially Soviet Jews, were also discriminated against in society, and often persecuted when they wanted to leave the Soviet Union for other lands. Many were denied outright the right to do so.

About the same time as the 27th Congress, Gorbachev showed that even dissidents could benefit from glasnost. He freed Jewish activist Anatoly Scharansky. Scharansky had spent nine years in prison accused of being an American spy, a charge that was never proven. In December 1986, the most famous Soviet dissident of all, sixty-five-year-old Andrei Sakharov, who was living in exile in Gorky, received a startling phone call from Moscow. "This is Gorbachev," said the blunt voice on the other end. The Soviet leader offered Sakharov, a famous physicist and winner of a Nobel Peace Prize, the freedom to return to Moscow from exile in Gorky, where he had spent the last seven years, often in poor health. Sakharov agreed to Gorbachev's offer, but only on the condition that the general secretary release a number of other political prisoners. In an unprecedented move that would have made Stalin turn in his grave, Gorbachev agreed to Sakharov's terms.

Sakharov continued to call out for the release of all political prisoners on his return to Moscow. However, he expressed his respect for Gorbachev and the changes he had brought about.

Glasnost picked up steam, like a speeding locomotive, and the response of conservatives and liberals became more dramatic. Conservatives wanted the brakes applied before the train leapt off the tracks. Liberals wanted the throttle opened full to speed the train on to what they saw as its final destination — a free and open society. By the fall of 1987, the lines of battle between these two groups had been firmly drawn. The two leaders of the opposing sides were ironically both close to Mikhail Gorbachev.

Yegor Ligachev, head of the conservatives, was Gorbachev's right-hand man in the Politburo. Gorbachev had broken the rules to elect him to the ruling body without first serving the traditional year's probation period. Now Ligachev's political power was second only to the General Secretary himself.

On the other side was Moscow party leader Boris Yeltsin. A strong supporter of perestroika, Yeltsin had grown frustrated with the slowness of reform. At a Central Committee meeting he had actually offered to resign if Gorbachev couldn't make good on his promises. Gorbachev handled the situation with tact. He urged Yeltsin to reconsider his statement. (Yeltsin did eventually resign.) A major showdown was brewing between Yeltsin and Ligachev and not even their diplomatic leader could stop it. The affair finally came to a shattering climax at a conference of the Communist party in July 1988.

If the 27th Party Congress two and a half years earlier had brought fresh air into the Soviet Union, at this conference these new breezes reached hurricane proportions. Millions of Soviet citizens sat glued to their television screens as delegate after delegate spoke the unspeakable, voicing both support and criticism for Gorbachev and his reforms.

At one point, a little-known delegate, Vladimir Milnikov, cried out for the dismissal of "those who in the past actively promoted the policy of stagnation." Gorbachev, with ironic humor, looked up from his place at the podium and asked the room, "Is he talking about me, or somebody else?"

Melnikov's reply was crisp and direct. He named two senior Politburo members and the editor of *Pravda*. Another disgruntled delegate, a machine-building plant director, minced no words about lazy bureaucrats in the system. "We don't need ministries," he told his fellow delegates. "But they should work and earn their keep. Let the ministers catch mice. If they don't, they don't eat."

But above all the fierce debating and name-calling, Mikhail Gorbachev was still firmly in charge. He jumped in to clear up a point or argue another, interrupting speakers as quickly as they interrupted each other. He skillfully played both sides of the fence — comforting conservatives and encouraging his fellow reformers.

But the reform-minded maverick of Soviet politics, Boris Yeltsin needed no encouragement. All eyes were on him as he made his way to the speaker's podium. He methodically put down some papers on the podium and began to speak. In ringing words, he condemned the Soviet leadership for dragging its feet in bringing about perestroika. Hundreds of delegates jeered and hissed Yeltsin. The Communist party's harshest critic had had enough. He began to gather together his papers, when Gorbachev stopped him from leaving and urged him to go on. "And if we have something to say, we'll say it too," Gorbachev added. Some of the anger left Yeltsin's voice and he backed down from his earlier stand. He asked the Party to give him another chance, to restore his good name and "rehabilitate" him.

Ligachev was on his feet. Yeltsin didn't deserve such treatment, he shouted. He hadn't learned from his mistakes, the conservative argued, and until he did, he didn't deserve to be a member of the power elite. The two men began a shouting match that electrified the other delegates and the entire television-viewing nation. In the end, Yeltsin lost. He had gone too far in his criticism of the system. He had failed to learn a valuable lesson from his leader, Gorbachev — that flexibility is a necessary trait in one who wishes to change the system from within. Gorbachev realized that Yeltsin had to be sacrificed, if he was to keep the careful balance between conservatives and liberals. Later he said, "Comrade Yeltsin's tragedy is that he simply didn't have it in him to solve all the problems and he resorted to loud and flashy talk instead."

Of course, Mikhail Gorbachev couldn't solve all the problems, either. Not yet at least. But he freely admitted his lack of success in an opening speech at the conference. Compared to previous speeches, this one was surprisingly short — only three and a half hours. While confessing that perestroika had been stalled and that the economy had reached a "dead end," Gorbachev called for more and greater reforms as the only solution. In his closing address he confidently proclaimed "We have the unqualified support of the people, who have adopted the policy of perestroika and will not tolerate its defeat."

Perhaps more than any resolution passed, the four-day conference itself was the best evidence that change was still sweeping across the Soviet Union, and that nothing would ever be quite the same again.

But there was another challenge that would have to be met if Gorbachev was to succeed. That challenge was not from within the Soviet Union but outside her borders. Mikhail Gorbachev would soon come face to face with the leader of his nation's leading global rival for over three decades — the United States of America.

9

The Rocky Path to Peace

SINCE THE DAYS of Joseph Stalin, the might of the Soviet Union's strength lay in her military and not her economy. Her superpower status was based on the tremendous number of nuclear warheads at her disposal, and on the Red Army, the largest land force in the world. Yet the country's inability to feed her people and provide them with consumer goods put the Soviet Union economically more on the level of a developing Third World country than on the level of a modern industrial nation like the United States.

Mikhail Gorbachev was well aware of this grim fact of life. He also realized that to build up the economy, funds had to be diverted from the military. For that to happen, the arms race with the West— where each side competed to outdo the other in building new weapons — had to come to a grinding halt. This arms race had been going on the end of World War II in

1945. For perestroika to take place, the Soviet Union's priorities had to be restructured as well as the rest of the society. The ability to build and create a better life for Soviet citizens had to take precedence over the need to maintain a huge military defense and build more nuclear weapons.

Gorbachev knew his task would not be easy. Allies during World War II, the United States and the Soviet Union, the two superpowers, had become bitter rivals in the years that followed. Stalin's takeover of numerous Eastern European countries in the postwar years put the United States on the defensive. The Soviets, on their side, saw themselves as alienated from the Western world, outcasts because of their revolutionary Communist beliefs. An iron curtain had descended that separated the Communist East, controlled from Moscow and the democratic West. Nikita Khrushchev tried to lessen tensions by calling for "peaceful coexistence" with the United States in 1956. But he also threatened the West that "we will bury you" and this did not convince the West that his peaceful intentions were sincere. Khrushchev later claimed he only meant the Soviet Union would "bury" the West economically, but his failed reforms and continued military buildup made this threat quite unlikely. The Brezhnev years saw some improvements in relations with the West, with a period of "detente" but there were few substantial changes in Soviet policy. And within the Soviet Union itself, there was no change in the unequal balance between guns and butter — or put another way, between military and consumer needs.

In 1985, Gorbachev began to reorganize priorities. Building up industry and raising crops were more important now than making weapons. The country couldn't afford to do both at the same time. Peace was necessary — not only to save the world from destruction but to save the Soviet Union from economic bankruptcy. However, Gorbachev saw one huge stumbling block on the path to peace.

In 1983, United States President Ronald Reagan had presented a plan to the American people, called the Strategic Defense Initiative (SDI). He claimed his plan would defend America from a nuclear attack. To the world, it quickly became known as "Star Wars," and it sounded like something straight out of that classic science fiction movie.

Laser and particle beams, according to the American president, would form a shield in outer space that would protect the United States from nuclear attack. These beams would be able to shoot down incoming missiles from the Soviet Union or any other country. Reagan claimed that SDI would make offensive weapons obsolete since the United States would not have to defend itself from nuclear attack.

Reagan's proposal was very controversial. Many people, including distinguished scientists, called it pure science fiction. They argued that the technology to create such a protective shield was not yet invented and that it would cost billions of dollars to develop. Even then, there was no guarantee that the system would actually work. One scientist called the pursuit of "Star Wars" as futile as "the search for perpetual motion." But Ronald Reagan had enough scientists who believed otherwise, and the presidential clout behind him to pursue his goal — at least for the moment.

Mikhail Gorbachev believed that "Star Wars" was a real threat to his ambitious economic plans and desire to slow the arms race. To allow the United States to develop such a defensive system, without then also developing a Soviet version was unthinkable. Yet Gorbachev could not afford to spend billions of rubles for such a project. His only choice, he believed, was to do everything in his power to persuade the United States to stop work on "Star Wars." To do this, he needed to meet the man behind the project, President Ronald Reagan.

The last time the leaders from the United States and the Soviet Union had come together was in 1979, when President Jimmy Carter met with General Secretary Leonid Brezhnev in Vienna, Austria. Since little had come from this meeting, the buildup of nuclear weapons had continued. United States-Soviet relations had become very strained soon thereafter when the Soviet Union invaded Afghanistan that same year, 1979. Gorbachev wanted to reopen communications. A summit was set for two days in November 1985. The chosen place was neutral Geneva, Switzerland. It would be the first time Gorbachev and Reagan met.

Few people were optimistic about the outcome. Reagan and Gorbachev were separated by twenty years in age, and they were also far apart in their attitudes. They had also exchanged heated accusations. Reagan had once called the Soviet Union an "evil empire." Gorbachev had referred to the United States as "the metropolitan center of imperialism" and saw Reagan as a "prisoner of the military-industrial complex," who was unable to prevent war, even if he wanted to. Everyone wondered what these two men could possibly agree on. How could they see past their differences and work together for peace?

On the morning of Monday, November 19, 1985, Ronald Reagan was the first to arrive at the charming, old country house on the shores of Lake Geneva where the summit talks would take place. The house had been vacated by its present owner, an Arab prince and his family. Reagan found a note from the prince asking him to please feed his son's tropical fish during his stay. The president was happy to do so, but was upset when one morning he found that one of the fish had died. He quickly sent an aide out to buy two more fish of the same species.

At ten A.M. Gorbachev arrived at the house in his limousine. The two men shook hands and went inside. Their introductory meeting was scheduled to be fifteen minutes long and involve only themselves and their two translators. The two men sat down in a small sitting room before a roaring fireplace. "Here we are," began Reagan. "Between us, we could come up with things that could bring peace for years to come." He suggested they extend the meeting so they could talk more without the interference of their advisers who were waiting in the wings. Gorbachev agreed. The advisers were not amused.

The conversation that followed offered little hope of peace. Reagan and Gorbachev argued about their support for the opposing sides in the military conflicts taking place in Nicaragua and in Afghanistan. While claiming to be serious about finding a solution to the Afghan war — which was draining the Soviet Union of troops and resources — Gorbachev gave no promise of a troop pullout.

At the discussion that afternoon the topic turned to arms control. Reagan defended his "Star Wars" program and offered to share its technology with the Soviets in "open laboratories." He claimed his space shield would make nuclear war impossible and eventually lead to world peace.

Gorbachev waited impatiently for the president to finish before he launched into his heated reply. "You can have dreams of peace," he retorted, "but we have to face reality. . . . We must reduce all weapons, not start on new ones." The Soviet leader's temper, usually under control, got away with him.

Reagan suggested they take a walk outside. "Ah! Fresh air may bring fresh ideas," replied Gorbachev. They strolled down to the pool house. Reagan pulled out some papers with specific proposals on arms control. The main proposal called for reducing nuclear weapons on both sides by half.

That was fine, responded Gorbachev, after looking over the proposals, but what about "Star Wars"? Reagan was not about to give up this program. So Gorbachev rejected the proposals and they were back at the beginning again. But both leaders accepted invitations to visit each other in their respective countries.

That evening the Reagans were the guests of the Gorbachevs at the Soviet mission in Geneva. The

Reuters/Bettmann Newsphotos

Soviet leader Mikhail Gorbachev and United States President
Ronald Reagan share a laugh at their 1985 summit meeting in
Geneva, Switzerland. Gorbachev, who has been called the
most innovative Soviet leader in the last forty years, has ushered
in a new era of friendship between the Soviet Union and
the United States.

dinner was pleasant, the small talk friendly, but both men must have wondered if the next day's talks would bring them any closer to some kind of agreement.

Wednesday morning's meeting again had few other participants aside from the two leaders. Gorbachev had such an intense, concentrated look when he listened that at times Reagan forgot he did not understand English. Occasionally Gorbachev had to hold up his hand for the president to slow down, so the translator could catch up with his words.

They were words that did not please the general secretary. Reagan urged Gorbachev to stop Soviet violation of basic human rights, urging him to release political dissenters from prison and allow more Soviet Jews to emigrate. Gorbachev countered that to him "human rights" were rights to be properly fed, have shelter and be provided with good health care. These were rights, he claimed, that many people in the United States — the poor and the homeless — did not have.

While their husbands argued, Nancy Reagan and Raisa Gorbachev met for tea and saw some of Geneva's sights together. Like her husband, Raisa Gorbachev was curious about everything, asked questions, and had a natural way of speaking that impressed those she met. Her public appearances were shown on Soviet television, where, for the first time, she was identified by name. Here, too, was a break from the traditions of the past. It was clear that Raisa Gorbachev would not be a "closet wife" as past Soviet first ladies had been. This was a far cry from even the short stint of Yuri Andropov, whose wife, until she appeared in public for the first time at his funeral, was not even known to exist!

Meanwhile the pressure for some kind of agreement between Reagan and Gorbachev was mounting. While the two leaders enjoyed a dinner hosted by the Reagans, that second evening, their advisers worked frantically on the wording of an agreement. Debates and arguments went on into the wee hours of the morning. Finally, at 4:45 A.M. the agreement was finished.

It was a four-and-a-half-page joint statement. Both sides agreed to reduce their nuclear weapons by half. Both sides agreed to speed up future arms-control negotiations. Yet the statement gave no directions on how to carry out the reductions or how each side would be able to verify them.

A more immediate and more positive decision was to renew cultural, educational, and athletic exchanges between the two countries; exchanges that had ended in 1980, after the Soviet invasion of Afghanistan.

Thursday morning Reagan and Gorbachev raised a toast to peace with glasses of champagne, said their farewells, and walked out into a lightly falling snow. Before leaving for home, Gorbachev was asked by a reporter about his "iron teeth." He replied good-humoredly, "It hasn't yet been confirmed. As of now, I'm still using my own teeth." The results of these first talks in Geneva were not spectacular. But the two men had met, gotten to know one another, and left with a new understanding and respect for each other. They had made a start and there was hope for the future.

Nearly a year later, in September 1986, Gorbachev wrote a letter to President Reagan, urging that they meet again to discuss arms control. The goal was to form a treaty both sides found acceptable. Reagan agreed and the summit was set for October 11 and 12, 1986 in Reykjavik, the capital of the island nation of Iceland. Iceland is located just north of Great Britain. *Time* magazine was to call this meeting "the most extraordinary bargaining session in the history of arms control."

This time Gorbachev was the one who brought along written proposals. At the first session on Saturday morning, he pulled some papers out of a briefcase and began to read them to a startled Reagan. The previously agreed upon 50 percent cut in nuclear weapons was still included, along with a wide-ranging number of new proposals for other missile reductions. Gorbachev wanted the 1972 Anti-Ballistic Missile (ABM) Treaty renewed for another ten years.

In essence, Gorbachev was also once more after "Star Wars," trying to include it with new weapons that the treaty would ban. By Saturday night, the Americans and Soviets were caught up in a game of nerves and bluff, trying to see who would give in first. Both sides finally settled on a maximum of 6,000 nuclear warheads each and agreed to eliminate all medium-range missiles in Europe. That still left the question of "Star Wars" undecided, to be dealt with during Sunday's session.

Sunday morning's meeting went smoothly, with most of the missile cuts approved by both sides. That afternoon Reagan and his secretary of state, George Shultz, agreed to extend the ABM Treaty for ten years but added that at the end of that time both sides would have to eliminate all nuclear missiles, would Gorbachev go for it? They wondered.

The final showdown came at 5:30 in the evening. Gorbachev and his foreign minister, Eduard Shevardnadze, listened to the final proposal from the United States. Extension of the ABM Treaty was acceptable, they said, but the Soviet leader wanted to state clearly that "Star Wars" be restricted to "laboratory research." Reagan shook his head. No, that would not do. He wanted the right to develop "Star Wars" beyond the laboratory. Then there could be no deal, Gorbachev replied bluntly.

The president wasn't ready to quit. "I made a promise to the American people that I would not trade away 'Star Wars,'" he told Gorbachev.

"But what is the function of a defense, if there are no missiles?" countered the Soviet.

"It's an insurance policy," replied Reagan, quoting the old Russian saying, *"Doveryai no proveryai,"* meaning, "Trust but verify."

Gorbachev was not impressed by Reagan's Russian wisdom. He wanted the assurance that "Star Wars" would not become reality and threaten his plans for rejuvenating his country. For Gorbachev, the draft treaty, as it stood, was unacceptable.

Finally, Reagan had enough. After fifteen hours of talks, they had only reached another deadlock. The president gathered up his papers and got up from the bargaining table.

On the short walk to Reagan's waiting limo, Gorbachev tried to repair the diplomatic damage, but it was too late.

"I think we can still deal," he told Reagan. "There is still time."

"I do not think you really wanted a deal," replied the president tersely.

"I do not know what else I could have done," said Gorbachev.

"You could have said yes."

There were no smiles or happy good-byes this time. The warmth of the first summit in Geneva was replaced by a chill from the second one in Reykjavik.

In his book, *Perestroika,* Gorbachev wrote that he told the president at Reykjavik "our meeting could not produce one winner: we will both either win or lose."

If Gorbachev was a loser, he did not look it on his return to Moscow. He received a hero's welcome from the members of the Politburo and the nation. For the second time he had gone one on one with the leader of the Western world and had shown himself to be tough, aggressive, and full of self-confidence.

President Reagan had also made a strong showing at the summit meeting with Gorbachev. But many critics at home in the United States wondered if this time he hadn't been set up, in a way, by the Soviet leader. Had Gorbachev deliberately tried to make him look like the "bad guy," the one who didn't want peace, all the while knowing Reagan would not give up his "Star Wars" program?

Or was Gorbachev simply trying to wear down Reagan's resistance to dropping the program, and if so, would this tactic work? Another summit might provide the answer. This time Ronald Reagan would have one big advantage. The meeting would be on his home turf.

10

"Gorby-Mania"

T HE PROMISE TO visit the United States that Mikhail Gorbachev made to Ronald Reagan in Geneva in 1985 was finally kept two years later. The Gorbachevs arrived in Washington, D.C. on December 8, 1987 for four days.

Expectations were high for the Soviet leader's first trip to the United States. The American people got their first close-up look at Gorbachev, however, even before he set foot in their country. While still in Moscow, he agreed to an unprecedented one-hour interview with American television journalist Tom Brokaw of the National Broadcasting Company (NBC) a week before his trip. The interview was conducted in the Kremlin's Council of Ministries and later broadcast on both American and Soviet television. Amazingly, Gorbachev answered all questions Brokaw put to him without first seeing them in advance, although NBC submitted a list of subjects to be covered.

The interview was a success for Gorbachev. He came across as a forceful and dazzling personality, as well as a crafty politician. Brokaw asked sharp questions, but often failed to follow them up or pursue a point when Gorbachev purposely was long-winded and evasive.

Among other things, Brokaw asked Gorbachev if he discussed important matters of state with his wife, Raisa. "We discuss everything," the Soviet leader answered. This exchange was the only part of the interview edited out of the Soviet broadcast, most likely because of conservative values in Soviet society, which frown on women participating in public life. It would have been too much of a shock for the Russian people to know that Raisa Gorbachev had such influence with their leader, or so the authorities thought.

Gorbachev showed his characteristic interest in people by asking a few questions himself. "What year were you born in?" he asked the newscaster. "Nineteen forty" replied the bemused Brokaw.

By the time the Gorbachevs arrived at Andrews Air Force Base outside Washington, D.C., on Monday, December 8, America was ready for them. The American press and public gave him a new nickname, "Gorby." It spoke volumes about Gorbachev's open personality and widespread popularity. Could anyone imagine calling Brehznev, "Breezy"?

On December 9, 1987, President Reagan officially welcomed the Gorbachevs on the South Lawn of the White House, while 1,000 invited guests watched.

The Soviet leader received a twenty-one gun salute and looked approvingly at the Soviet flag held alongside the American Stars and Stripes by a Marine color guard.

On this, their third meeting, the two leaders' acquaintance deepened. They entered the president's Oval Office for a ninety-minute private talk in front of a roaring fire. They immediately agreed to call each other "Ron" and "Mikhail." They discussed human rights that morning. Reagan wanted Gorbachev to let more Soviet Jews emigrate. Gorbachev wanted Reagan to first do something about the thousands of homeless people that inhabited the streets of American cities.

These old differences, however, didn't get in the way of a new treaty they signed that afternoon. It called for banning short and middle-range nuclear missiles on both sides. It was a historic moment, the way to it paved, in part, by the deadlocks of Geneva and Reykjavik. It was the first treaty of its kind to not merely control, but to actually eliminate, an entire category of nuclear missiles. After signing the English and Russian translations of the treaty in the East Room of the White House, the two men, at Gorbachev's suggestion, exchanged silver pens.

The issue of world peace was easy to agree on in general. But there were many trouble spots in the world and there were specific disagreements between the two men about them. At a second meeting in the Oval Office, Gorbachev refused Reagan's suggestion for an immediate withdrawal from Afghanistan. He proposed instead a gradual withdrawal over a year's time, but only on the condition that the United States would end its aid to the anti-Communist rebels in Afghanistan also.

Gorbachev also met with several specially invited prominent Americans — from all walks of life — at the Soviet embassy. He impressed everyone from former Secretary of State Henry Kissinger to Yoko Ono, John Lennon's widow. There was also a formal state dinner at the White House, where entertainment was provided by Texas pianist Van Cliburn. No stranger to the Soviet Union, Cliburn had won the first International Tchaikovsky Competition in Moscow nearly thirty years before. Cliburn charmed the Gorbachevs with his playing of the favorite Russian song, "Moscow Nights." Mikhail and Raisa Gorbachev led the Soviet delegation in a sing-along.

On the third day of his visit Gorbachev met with nine congressional leaders, finding time to exchange some private words with Senator Robert Dole, who was then running for the Republican presidential nomination against Vice-President George Bush. A short meeting and stroll across the White House lawn with the president followed. In the meantime, the two first ladies were getting reacquainted.

Gorbachev showed his streak of independence on the last day of his visit. He was late for a final talk with the President. His long motorcade of limousines speeded through downtown Washington. Vice-President George Bush accompanied him to this meeting. As the two men gazed out their bulletproof windows at the crowds along the boulevards, Bush remarked that it would be wonderful to meet all those people in person.

Gorbachev acted on the idea immediately. "Stop the car," he commanded the driver. To Bush's amazement, Gorbachev stepped out into the crowded street. Panic broke out in the motorcade. KGB agents in the front limos slammed on their brakes and backed up. Secret Service agents in other cars jumped out and raced to the scene.

Gorbachev paid no attention to the pandemonium he had caused. His attention was focused on the crowd of surprised Americans in the street. "I want to say hello to you," he said with a smile and began shaking hands across the wooden barricades.

As the Soviet leader spoke of peace, the crowd applauded. "We were struck with awe," said one young bystander later.

When Gorbachev finally arrived at the White House, a joint statement was waiting for his signature. The statement, citing areas of agreement between Gorbachev and Reagan, was a fitting end to a remarkable four days. It showed that the relationship between two very different people — the Soviets and the Americans — was finally improving. Despite disagreements, particularly over Reagan's "Star Wars" project, the two leaders vowed to keep talking, keep working toward abolishing all nuclear weapons and keep trying to achieve world peace. The Gorbachevs left Washington with the promise that the Reagans would be their guests in Moscow the next year.

Within half a year—in June 1988—the Reagans flew to the Soviet Union for their first visit. This time there were no major treaties to sign, no specific proposals to consider. Nevertheless, those four days were important symbolically. One of America's most staunchly conservative presidents had set foot on Soviet soil and had thereby brought renewed hope for friendship and peace between the two countries.

Gorbachev wanted Reagan to see the Soviet Union firsthand. "Aware of your fondness for Russian proverbs, let me add another one to your collection," said Gorbachev as he welcomed Reagan to Moscow. "It is better to see once than to hear a hundred times."

Gorbachev took Reagan for a walk in Red Square, just outside the Kremlin walls. President Reagan later reported everyone he met there was "warm and enthusiastic." Gorbachev saw a little boy in his mother's arms, picked him up, and asked him to "shake hands with Grandfather Reagan."

If his age, seventy-seven, slowed the president down at times during his visit, he still put on a good show for his Soviet hosts. He talked openly and often to the press and the people and upheld his reputation as the "great communicator." He even spoke to students at Gorbachev's old alma mater, Moscow State University. "Your generation is living in one of the most exciting, hopeful times in Soviet history," he said. "It is a time when the first breath of freedom stirs the air and the heart beats to the accelerated rhythm of hope."

Reagan also met with a group of American exchange students. He told them of the need to increase the number of students on such programs, so that many more young people could get to know each other's country better.

Gorbachev still disliked Reagan's demands on human rights, but in the end, the tone of goodwill prevailed. The two men signed seven minor treaties and the Reagan visit strengthened Soviet-American relations even further. *Time* magazine claimed, "It may prove, when history looks back, to be Reagan's finest hour."

As for Mikhail Gorbachev, his "finest hours" still seemed ahead of him. There was much yet to do, both at home and abroad. With only six months remaining in Reagan's term, Gorbachev was already looking forward to meeting the next United States president and moving forward on the arms issue. That opportunity would come before the year was over.

11

Triumph and Tragedy

THE LAST TIME a Soviet leader had spoken to the General Assembly at the United Nations in New York City was back in 1960. That leader was Nikita Khrushchev; and his speech had been startling. Like Gorbachev, he had promised sweeping changes in the Soviet Union and called for world peace. It was a fine speech but unlike Gorbachev, Khrushchev's subsequent actions were not as inspiring as his words. By the time he was deposed from power four years later, about the only thing people remembered from his visit to the United Nations was that he pounded a table angrily with his shoe when another delegate said something he didn't like.

In December 1988, Mikhail Gorbachev was determined to do better. He also spoke before the General Assembly, but his bold words were backed by strong, swift actions, both at home and abroad. His visit to New York City, the United States' largest and most famous city, was further highlighted by once again meeting both with Ronald Reagan, the outgoing president, and the new president-elect, George Bush.

In the weeks before his visit, no one knew for sure what Gorbachev would say at the United Nations. Many American officials in the Reagan administration were apprehensive about the four-day visit. Some thought it would be strictly a show for the media, the kind of glamorous event that the Gorbachevs, both Mikhail and Raisa, were now quite adept at. Others believed Gorbachev would make some stunning announcement about arms control that would upstage the United States, thus forcing the Americans to make more concessions toward nuclear disarmament than they were prepared for.

The people of New York City had another reason to be anxious. Gorbachev was visiting their city at the height of the holiday season when the city streets were mobbed with Christmas shoppers, tourists — and cars. The Soviet leader's forty-five car motorcade wound its way through the busy streets at least once during the evening rush hour, causing a massive traffic jam, or gridlock. New Yorkers quickly came up with a name for this phenomenon — "Gorbilock."

Six thousand police officers assigned to protect Gorbachev and to keep crowds under control also had to contend with the Soviet leader's unpredictability. Gorbachev was scheduled, for example, to drive through Times Square, Broadway's famous theater district. Would the impish Gorby pop out of his limo as he had in Washington, causing havoc for police and security agents alike? The New York City police had to be prepared for anything.

When he arrived at Kennedy International Airport on the afternoon of December 6, Gorbachev said he hoped his visit would inject a new enthusiasm into Soviet-American relations. "We shall be sharing our concerns and our interests."

The next morning, Gorbachev got down to business. His speech to the United Nations General Assembly was a blockbuster and a dramatic breakthrough. He announced that the Soviet Union would reduce its military force in Eastern Europe by 500,000 men and 10,000 tanks, about 10 percent of its total military manpower and over one-fourth of its tanks there. There were no pre-conditions that Gorbachev required the United States to meet in order for this to happen, although later he said, "We do hope that the United States and the Europeans also take some steps" in the same direction.

But that wasn't all. Gorbachev vowed that new laws in 1989 in the Soviet Union itself would not only grant freedom of expression and assembly but actually prohibit "any form of persecution" of Soviet citizens for their political or religious beliefs. He also promised that all Soviet emigrés, Jewish and otherwise, would be allowed to leave the country, even those previously denied exit visas because of alleged knowledge of government secrets.

Gorbachev outlined a new proposal to end the Afghanistan war, calling for a cease-fire on January 1, 1989 between the rebels and the Soviet-supported

Communist government. The Soviet leader proposed that United Nations forces monitor the cease-fire.

He spoke of the goals he had on his agenda for future meetings with President-Elect Bush. They included a treaty on a 50-percent reduction in strategic offensive weapons, the elimination of chemical weapons, and negotiations on the reduction of conventional arms in Europe.

"I would like to believe," concluded Gorbachev, "that our hopes will be matched by our joint effort to put an end to an era of wars, confrontation, and regional conflicts, to aggressions against nature, to the terror of hunger and poverty as well as to political terrorism. This is our common goal and we can only reach it together."

It was clear to many Western observers that part of Gorbachev's motive in reducing the Soviet military presence in Eastern Europe was to redirect resources to strengthen the weak Soviet economy. But it was equally clear that his commitment to world peace was very genuine and that he sincerely desired the reduction of tensions between the superpowers and their allies. The Reagan administration's immediate reaction was one of "hearty approval," but signaled no similar troop cuts from their side. It was a transitional time for the United States. With one president about to leave and a new one about to take office, no new policy could be set, a situation Gorbachev seemed to understand and accept.

Thunderous applause followed Gorbachev as he left the United Nations to take the ferry to nearby Governor's Island. Here, he met for lunch with Ronald Reagan and George Bush in the Admiral's House, a twenty-seven-room Georgian mansion. Over wild-mushroom ravioli and veal with smoked quail and lobster sauce, the three men and their aides recalled past diplomatic triumphs and talked of future ones. According to *New York Times* reporter, Steven V. Roberts, it was "more like a holiday party among old friends than a negotiating session."

George Bush played down his role in the meeting. When asked by reporters what he thought of Gorbachev's speech, he replied with a laugh, "I support what the president says. I'm vice-president."

"That's one of the best answers of the year," quipped Gorbachev.

Before it was over, Reagan presented Gorbachev with a framed photograph of the two men walking during their first summit meeting in Geneva. The inscription read, "We have walked a long way together to clear a path for peace."

After a short stop before the Statue of Liberty with his two hosts, where photographers took pictures of the three men, Gorbachev joined his wife for an afternoon tour of the city. Everywhere they went they drew crowds of admiring and curious New Yorkers.

One bicycle messenger spotted the Soviet leader visiting the New York Stock Exchange. He was ecstatic. "I just saw Gorbachev. I'll never wash my eyes again!" he said.

As their Soviet limousine motorcade slowly drove through Manhattan's theater district, Gorbachev signaled to his driver to stop in front of the Winter Garden Theatre where the musical *Cats* was playing.

He climbed out with Raisa and raised his arms in a Victory salute to the crowd. The people went wild. "Gorby! Gorby! Gorby!" they chanted loudly. But when the Soviet leader started to advance forward for a few handshakes, his security agents formed a protective wall around him and stopped him in his tracks. This didn't prevent a handful of resourceful New Yorkers from ducking under the police barriers and slipping past the KGB agents to shake hands with their new idol.

One high school senior from Connecticut summed up the feelings of many people. "It was a once-in-a-lifetime chance," he remarked later. "It was a rush."

The Gorbachevs made a second stop in front of New York's most celebrated department store, Bloomingdale's. By now, the rest of the motorcade knew what to expect, and stopped as their limo did.

Yet while Gorbachev was savoring his greatest triumph in New York, the starkest of tragedies was unfolding back home in Armenia, one of the Soviet Union's fifteen republics. About noon on Wednesday, December 9, an earthquake struck without warning in northern Soviet Armenia. At first, reports of the quake were that it was minor, but as the hours passed, it became increasingly clear to the world that this was a natural disaster of enormous proportions. At 6.9 on the Richter scale it was said to be the worst earthquake to hit the region in a thousand years, and one of the most serious disasters ever seen in the Soviet Union.

Mikhail Gorbachev now faced a critical decision. Although his visit to New York was important, he also realized that if he stayed another day — enjoying American hospitality while people were dying and suffering at home — he and his government would appear to be unfeeling and callous. Gorbachev made up his mind quickly. Shortly after midnight on Thursday morning, Soviet Foreign Minister Shevardnadze announced that the Gorbachevs were canceling their subsequent trips to Cuba and Great Britain. They were going home.

At Kennedy Airport before leaving, the Soviet leader expressed his gratitude to New York and to the entire nation, adding that, "The road ahead will be tough, but we will go ahead . . . and we will — I believe — be building on what has been achieved if we act as we have been acting, and also maybe add something new."

Once back in the Soviet Union, Gorbachev left for Armenia at once. With Raisa, he visited the worst-hit towns and cities of Armenia to talk with officials, assess the damage, and try to comfort survivors. But this was not to be the glowing reception he had received in New York. A number of Armenians greeted Gorbachev with jeers, whistles, and angry questions. They were not only upset by the slow response to their tragedy from Moscow — for material help did not arrive as quickly as Gorbachev had — but to the government's indifference to their long-standing border dispute with the neighboring republic of Azerbaijan.

Gorbachev was both shocked and angered by this chilly reception. He couldn't believe that some Armenians were letting political differences overshadow this national tragedy. The Armenians, for their part, believed that it was Gorbachev who was putting politics before saving people's lives.

There were also other problems. The Soviet Union was totally unprepared for this greatest of disasters. There wasn't enough rescue equipment or competent people to organize the rescue effort. The airport nearest the most devastated city of Leninakan was completely incapable of handling the heavy stream of incoming aid. Two transport planes crashed before landing, killing many passengers and destroying cargo sent to aid the rescue. The lost hours and days meant death for hundreds of victims trapped under tons of rubble from fallen buildings.

Perhaps the most devastating revelation was that many of these buildings had collapsed — causing many deaths — because of shoddy construction. Corrupt and careless builders and officials had allowed the illegal construction of buildings too tall for the earthquake zone. Furthermore, sand had often been substituted for cement in the mortar, resulting in weak foundations that crumbled in the quake, while the unused cement had been sold by builders for a profit on the black market. All of this had gone on during the days of the Brezhnev regime. The sins of the past had come back to haunt the present, as Mikhail Gorbachev was painfully aware.

But amid the tragedy something unexpected also happened to bring new hope. At the United Nations, Gorbachev had spoken of a world where people cared about one another, regardless of their nationality or beliefs. Now, the world responded, showing that this hope could indeed exist. Aid poured in from every corner of the globe. Within days, the Armenian Relief Society in the United States raised over three million dollars in aid. Paramedics, search teams, and trauma physicians from Florida, Virginia, and other states rushed to the Soviet Union to help with the rescue effort. Help also came from Great Britain, Scandinavia, Israel, Latin America, Japan, and even Afghanistan. Afghan children donated blood to help quake victims.

Yet, perhaps the greatest change was not that the aid was given, but that it was asked for in the first place. The Soviet Union, which previously had never admitted that it experienced catastrophes, had not accepted foreign aid on such a scale since the end of World War II. During the week at the United Nations, Gorbachev had reached out to the world from a position of strength. The earthquake now showed the Soviets reaching out from a desperate need. As one Soviet expert said, the earthquake "serves to validate Gorbachev's notion of the need for the Soviet Union to become part of the larger world community."

As aid poured in, news of the crisis went out with an openness previously unknown in the Soviet Union. Foreign journalists, including Gorbachev interviewer Tom Brokaw, were allowed to enter the worst-hit areas of Armenia and travel freely to report what they saw. Of course, Gorbachev's motives were, to an extent, self-serving. The way to keep foreign aid coming in was to keep the earthquake's devastating aftermath in the news. Yet, the contrast with a more repressive and secretive Soviet past was startling. A previous earthquake in the republic of Turkmen forty years earlier had killed 100,000 people, four times the estimated victims in Armenia. However, the event received only a scant paragraph in the party newspaper at the time, and its full scope was only revealed to the West in 1988.

There was still the problem of the regional conflict to contend with. Gorbachev was realistic. His own welcome had been chilly, so he sent Prime Minister Nikolai I. Ryzhkov to be his representative. A skillful diplomat, Ryzhkov won the confidence and respect of the Armenians by improving the rescue operations and staying on the scene twenty-four hours a day for several weeks. He proved to be a positive buffer between the Armenians and the Soviet government in Moscow.

The earthquake was a tragedy, but one that brought the Soviet people together as no other event had since World War II. It gave dramatic proof that glasnost had made it hard for anyone to imagine the system returning to the secretive, repressive ways of the past. The earthquake had exposed the weaknesses and stagnation of recent Soviet society. Much of the credit for this openness had to be given to one man — Mikhail Gorbachev. In one month — December 1988 — he had tasted both triumph and tragedy. Yet he had emerged from both experiences with the respect and admiration of the world.

12

The Road Ahead

IN HIS FIRST four years in power Mikhail Gorbachev has inspired his countrymen and created a positive image of leadership that has excited the world's imagination and brought the United States to the bargaining table in an unprecedented series of summit talks. His report card up until now has generally been a good one. He has earned high marks even when his actions haven't always measured up to his rhetoric.

When things have gone wrong — as they did at Chernobyl and the Armenian earthquake — he has shown the ability to act sensibly under pressure, a true test of great leadership for many people. Gorbachev has sometimes, even managed to turn liabilities into assets. However, the road ahead is fraught with problems and challenges that will require all his energy, political wisdom, and statesmanship.

Perhaps the most immediate of these problems is the one he has vowed to set straight since he first came to power — the economy. Perestroika has not, in the short-term, been successful and frustrating millions of Soviet citizens, many of whom enthusiastically supported Gorbachev's efforts to radically restructure the economy.

The New Year in Russia is a time for celebrating, but there was little to celebrate as 1989 began. Shortages of foods and other consumer goods hit an all-time high. One Soviet newspaper put it bluntly: "Shortages attack us literally from all sides. It seems that soon it will be difficult to name an item that doesn't fall into a shortage category."

Many people, inspired by Gorbachev's bold call for more free enterprise, find themselves trapped between the old economy and the new one. They have bold, new ideas, but the means to carry them out lag behind, caught up in bureaucratic red tape and the stagnation of the old system. Consumers are frustrated and angry. They hear the bright promises of their leader, want to believe them, and are deeply disappointed to be facing the same long lines at their local stores and the same empty shelves when they finally get inside. "Recently all you hear is perestroika, glasnost," wrote one villager from the Ural Mountains, in a letter to the editor. "But what has changed?"

While perestroika has appeared to fail, so far, glasnost has succeeded to a certain degree. There is more freedom of speech and thought in the Soviet Union than perhaps ever before. Yet much of this has not improved people's attitude. The more people can voice the things that they are dissatisfied with, the more keenly aware they are of the magnitude of those problems and the inability of the Soviet system to solve them.

"Gorbachev has let the genie out of the bottle," claimed former White House National Security Adviser Zbigniew Brzezinski, "and his successors will not be able to stuff if back in. . . .Gorbachev's legacy is going to be a Soviet Union in protracted turmoil." One area where glasnost is creating serious problems within the Soviet Union is that of native nationalism. There are over two hundred and fifty different ethnic groups in the fifteen republics that make up the Union of Soviet Socialist Republics, or Soviet union. Many of these groups have their own culture, language, and national identity. As we have seen, some of them, like the Armenians, are actively protesting Soviet interference in their lives and their conflicts with their neighbors. When Gorbachev couldn't satisfactorily settle the land dispute the Armenians had with the Muslim people of Azerbaijan, satisfactorily, his popularity in Armenia plummeted. The resolution of this long-standing blood feud will not be easy, if it can be resolved at all.

Even more pressing for Gorbachev is the liberating movement presently under way in the Baltic states of Estonia, Latvia, and Lithuania. These small republics on the eastern European border of the Soviet Union were once independent countries, but came under Soviet dominance in 1940. In recent months, the people and government officials in these tiny republics have called for greater political and economical independence from Moscow. Gorbachev has tried to satisfy their demands while allaying the fears of Kremlin hardliners. How much longer he can keep this uneasy balance remains to be seen.

Perhaps the greatest threat to Gorbachev, however, is one much closer to home — a threat posed by his own colleagues in the Politburo and Central Committee of the Communist party. Up until now Gorbachev has managed to walk a thin line between the liberals and conservatives within the Party. He has been secure in the knowledge that those who have opposed him — both from the left and right — have neither been united nor had a viable program to offer as an alternative. However, this could change. The Soviet leader's failures may give these dispensable rivals the confidence and strength they need to oust him and make him a scapegoat for everything that is wrong in the Soviet Union. On the other hand, his successes may threaten their own political power and undermine the special privileges that they have enjoyed since the days of Leonid Brezhnev. So, ironically, Gorbachev's success could also lead to his undoing.

Through all this, Gorbachev can look back at the fate of Nikita Khrushchev, the one man before him who tried to change the system. When Khrushchev's bold, but often haphazard reforms failed, the Politburo quickly removed him from power and forced him into early retirement. Could the same thing happen to Gorbachev? It could, but many Soviet experts think that Gorbachev is a much smarter politician than Khrushchev was and so far has shown far better judgment. Gorbachev has been careful not to go too far too fast in his actions and has worked hard not to alienate those members of the power elite who helped put him in power and whom he needs to stay there. So what does the future hold for Mikhail Gorbachev and the mighty nation he governs? There are three scenarios that could happen in the years ahead. The first is that Gorbachev will fail to fulfill his ambitious goals; this will lead to increased dissatisfaction among the Soviet people and his eventual removal from power by the members of the Politburo. A weaker but more manageable politician might then replace him in order to return to the old ways of governing. Such a scenario would be disastrous for the Soviet Union and a threat to world peace as Soviet-American relations would surely return to the dismal and tense days of the Cold War.

If, on the other hand, Gorbachev succeeds in his plan for perestroika, as some astute observers such as former President Jimmy Carter think possible, Gorbachev could remain in power as general secretary into the 21st century. A very different kind of Soviet leader, Joseph Stalin, consolidated his power at the age of fifty and then remained in power until his death more than twenty years later.

There is a third possible scenario. In the face of growing opposition and failed reforms, Mikhail Gorbachev might save his political career by sacrificing his own goals. He could reverse his own policies and take a new conservative line. If he were to do this and go back on the progressive agenda he has laid down, he would lose his bright image in the West, if not at home, and go down in the history books as worse than a failure. He will have betrayed himself, his people, and the world.

Which scenario will come true? Only time will tell. The bolder Gorbachev becomes in his efforts to create a new Soviet state based on democratic principles, free enterprise, and peaceful foreign relations, the harder it will be for him to try to renounce them later. The higher he sets his goals, the more vulnerable he becomes as a target for his enemies; but the greater will be his victory, if he succeeds.

Perhaps former United States President Carter sums up best the attitudes of many Americans towards this phenomenal leader. "Gorbachev has already set an innovative and ambitious agenda. . . . How much of this effort is sincere and how much is designed for propaganda remains to be seen."

So, we in the West sit, watch, and wait. If Gorbachev holds good to his promises for a new, strong, and peace-loving Soviet Union, the time for waiting will be over. The United States and other countries will be inspired to demonstrate their own faith in themselves and their principles. As Gorbachev himself has written, ". . . if the Russian word perestroika has easily entered the international lexicon, this is due to more than just interest in what is going on in the Soviet Union. Now the whole world needs restructuring, progressive development, a fundamental change."

13

The View from Proletarskii

I T WAS A warm January day in the unusually mild winter of 1989 in the city of Moscow. In his apartment in the Proletarskii District, old Ivan Ivanovich couldn't recall another winter like it in over a decade. It was unseasonably warm and Ivan didn't like it one bit. There was something wrong when the snow wasn't piled high along the streets and the thermometer refused to dip below zero for days at a time.

It was almost as warm as it was that memorable day in April 1985 when Mikhail Gorbachev walked the streets of Proletarskii, shaking hands and talking to everyone he met. What a day that had been, Ivan remembered with a smile. He thought back to how he had spoken out boldly to the new general secretary in front of the entire neighborhood. They were all afraid for him for speaking out so.

Now such fear would be unthinkable. Glasnost, the new openness, had taken care of that. A lot had changed in the Soviet Union in four years. And yet some things had hardly changed at all. The street Ivan and his family lived on was still run-down and the houses and factories were still in disrepair. But the spirit of the people had changed. Many were excited by what was happening and hopeful about the future. True, many others were frustrated and unhappy with the slowness of the changes. But they all *cared* about what happened. They all felt a part of something bigger than themselves.

As Ivan Ivanovich shifted his leg on the footstool in front of his armchair he felt a twinge of pain. He had changed too, but not for the better. In the last four years his arthritis had gotten worse. Yet, old as he was, his spirit was still young — younger than it had been in twenty years. This Mikhail Gorbachev had been an excellent physician for his spirit, if not for his uncooperative body.

Ivan opened up the afternoon newspaper. There was another article about the second earthquake to rock the Soviet Union in a month. This one had struck the central Asian republic of Tadzhikistan. A mudslide caused by the earthquake left nearly three hundred people dead. It was nowhere near as damaging as the Armenian earthquake, but it was another blow to the morale of the Soviet people.

There was better news on the political pages. Boris N. Yeltsin, the former maverick mayor of Moscow was making a political comeback. Written off after his bitter defeat at the Communist Party Conference the previous summer, Yeltsin had now accepted a popular draft from the public to be a candidate for the new National Congress of Deputies. How Yeltsin would fare and how much support he would receive from his former mentor Mikhail Gorbachev remained to be seen. But Ivan wished him luck. He had always liked the forward-looking, outspoken boss of his city. Ivan believed Gorbachev needed such a man to keep pushing him forward in the right direction. Further down on the page Ivan saw a small article about a less-popular political figure. His name was Yuri M. Churbonov, and he had been Leonid Brezhnev's son-in-law. As the second highest-ranking Soviet police official from 1980 to 1984, Churbonov had accepted bribes and used his high position to make himself rich. A military court had sentenced him to twelve years in a labor camp for his crimes of corruption. It gave Ivan great satisfaction to see the crimes of those in power during the Brezhnev years finally coming to light and Gorbachev's government prosecuting corrupt officials.

On the next page there was another pledge from the general secretary to make more military cuts in the Soviet budget. That was good news. So was the impending end to the Afghanistan war that had taken the lives of thousands of young Soviet soldiers. The last troops were scheduled to come home in February.

With all this money being taken from the military and put into industry and agriculture, Ivan thought, you would think the economy would be booming. But such was not the case, he had to admit. Shortages in consumer products were as bad as they had ever been. Ivan scanned an article written by an economics expert. The expert predicted that another six years would pass before perestroika made any real improvements in the average Soviet citizen's standard of living.

Six years! Ivan thought that in six years he might not even be around. He put down the newspaper. Some news it was better not to know about. What a change from the old days, mused Ivan. Then we knew next to nothing about what was going on in our country. Now we know everything. Ivan could not decide which was worse.

Suddenly he heard the front door of the apartment slam. His grandson Peter was home from school. Ivan was pleased. He was enjoying Peter more and more, as he grew older. At ten, the boy was tall and good-looking. Almost as good-looking as Ivan himself had been at the same age.

"How was school?" he asked, as Peter entered the living room and plopped his books on the coffee table.

"All right," he said.

"What did you learn today?" asked Ivan.

"All about Stalin," said Peter. He was obviously more interested in finding a snack in the kitchen than answering his grandfather's questions.

"And what did the teacher say about Stalin?" Ivan demanded.

"She said he killed thousands and thousands of Soviet citizens before the Great Patriotic War," said Peter. "Grandfather, is that true?" Ivan nodded his head solemnly, thinking of the years before World

War II. He remembered friends from the 1930s who had died senselessly by Stalin's orders during that time of terror. "It is true," he said. "But for a long time no one in our country wanted to admit it."

Peter stared at his grandfather. He had forgotten all about his snack for the moment. "Grandfather, how could he do such a thing, to his own people?"

"He was, in many ways, an evil man," replied Ivan. "He did some good things for our country, but he also did much evil."

"When I grow up, I'm going to do only good things," said Peter. "I'm going to help people, like General Secretary Gorbachev."

Ivan smiled. He could think of far worse models for his grandson to have than their leader. And few that were better.

"Well, if you are going to do all these things, you'll have to keep your strength up," said Ivan. "Now go into the kitchen and find yourself a cookie or two that your mother baked this morning, before she comes home and catches you!"

Peter needed no second invitation. He tore into the kitchen at once. Ivan chuckled and then turned his attention to the window. He thought he heard people's voices and some commotion in the street outside. He began to get up, but then remembered his arthritis.

"Peter," he called out. "When you find your cookies, come here and look out the window for me."

Peter came back into the room, a large brown cookie held firmly in one hand. Peter went to the window and gazed out. "There are people in the street," he said "Lots of them. And there are television cameras, and a man is talking into a microphone."

Could it be the general secretary coming back for a second visit to the neighborhood? Ivan forced himself up from his chair. Ignoring the pain in his legs, he hobbled over to the window. No, there was no man with a red birthmark on his head in the crowd below. However, the crowd was nearly as large and excited as the one that gathered around Gorbachev nearly four years earlier.

At that moment, Nikolai and Valentina came in, filled with enthusiasm. Peter stuffed the last of his cookie into his mouth as his mother entered the room.

"Father!" exclaimed Nikolai. "Have you heard the news?"

"I've heard nothing," replied Ivan, a bit irritated. "But I've seen plenty. What's going on out there?"

"One of the local television stations is filming a documentary about Proletarskii District," said Valentina. "They want to expose some of the problems we have here so the whole country can see. They are interviewing factory workers and other people in the neighborhood for their program. Isn't that exciting?"

"Maybe now some of those things you told the general secretary about four years ago will be corrected," said Nikolai.

"Oh, grandfather!" exclaimed Peter, swallowing the last of his cookie, "you must go out and talk to the reporter! Just like you talked to Mr. Gorbachev!"

"Oh, yes," chimed in Valentina. "This time they'll put you on television for longer than before. You'll be a star!"

Ivan smiled and shook his gray head. "No, no," he said. "Once in the spotlight is enough for me. I'm an old man. It is up to you and Nikolai and Peter to speak up now. This is your time. Our country is changing, and you must do your part to help it along."

Nikolai looked at his father with surprise, but then his eyes softened as he smiled at the old man with warmth and love. "All right, father," he said at last. "We will go out and speak for you . . . and ourselves."

"You'd better hurry," urged Ivan. "That television crew won't stay out there all night."

"We won't be long," promised Valentina. "And I'll fix your dinner as soon as we get back."

Ivan waved his hand impatiently. "Dinner can wait," he said "but the television cameras can't."

After they left, Ivan settled back into his armchair. It looked as if glasnost had come to Proletarskii with as much fanfare as Gorbachev had. It had taken awhile, but change was coming gradually to their run-down neighborhood. And Ivan Ivanovich thought with pride that maybe he had played some small part in bringing about this change.

He closed his tired eyes and thought about the future. He thought of a future in his country where people were free to speak their minds and fill their stomachs and live as well as people did in the United States. In this future, people were allowed to vote for whomever they wanted and officials they elected would be held accountable directly to the people who elected them. Some of Ivan's dreams were already coming true. Others were still little more than dreams. He, Ivan Ivanovich, would not live to see all these things come true. But young Peter might. That thought was somehow a great comfort to the old man.

He opened his eyes and felt refreshed. He began to reach for the newspaper again, but spied the textbook on the table where Peter had dropped it. He picked it up and read the title on the cover — *A History of the Soviet Union*. The copyright date was 1988. Ivan had the distinct feeling this history would be very different from anything that had been published previously. For once, he hoped to read the story of his country as it actually happened, not as officials dictated it. Truth — that is what would make them strong and free. Ivan Ivanovich opened the book to the first chapter and began to read.

GLOSSARY

capitalism — an economic system in which most of the industries and businesses in a country are owned privately, rather than by the government

collectivization — the organization of people or things as a group or whole. In the 1930s, the government of the Soviet Union *collectivized* the country's agriculture, creating farming *collectives* where once there were individual farmers.

communism — a system based on property ownership by a community as a whole or by the state. Communist societies are characterized by Communist Party control over all political and social activity and by central planning of the economy.

democracy — a philosophy of government based on the belief that all people should have the same rights and freedoms. Citizens of a democracy exercise power through elected representatives.

détente — a relaxation of tensions or strained relations between nations

embargo — a restriction placed upon trade or commerce by a government or law

fascism — a philosophy of government based on the belief that power should be exercised by a dictator and that any opposition and criticism should be suppressed by force. Fascist governments place primary importance on nation or race and very little on individual freedoms and rights.

glasnost — the Russian word for "openness"

imperialistic — supporting or practicing imperialism. Imperialism is the policy by which one nation extends its rule or authority over another, often by force, but also by economic controls or cultural influence.

Kremlin — the enclosed compound in Moscow which houses the Soviet government and a number of other buildings used for state ceremonies and business. The word is also used to describe the Soviet government in general, as in ''The Kremlin announced...''

Komsomol — a Young Communist League. About half the students in the Soviet Union belong to one of a few such leagues, which teach Communist Party values, among other things.

militarism — dominance by the military class or its ideals; a policy of maintaining a large military establishment in a state of aggressive readiness

''peaceful coexistence'' — the state of relations between countries that live without hostility despite differing values, governments, and ways of life

perestroika — the Russian word for ''restructuring''

Politburo — the executive committee and top decision-making body in a Communist party

propaganda — ideas, information, rumors, and even untruths that are spread to persuade others of the rightness of one's cause or point of view

rhetoric — literally, the art of speaking or writing effectively. The word is more commonly used to describe a type or mode of speech in which sophisticated, sometimes insincere, language is used to make a point.

Other books you might enjoy reading

1. Butson, G. Thos. *Gorbachev — A Biography.* Stein & Day, 1985.

2. Gorbachev, Mikhail. *Perestroika: New Thinking for Our Country and the World.* Harper & Row, 1987.

3. Klose, Kevin. *Russia and the Russians: Inside the Closed Society.* W.W. Norton, 1984.

4. Resnick, Abraham. *The Union of Soviet Socialist Republics.* Part of *Enchantment of the World* series. Childrens Press, 1984.

5. Salisbury, Harrison E. *Black Night, White Snow: Russia's Revolutions 1905-1917.* Da Capo Press, 1981.

6. Shipler, David K. *Russia: Broken Idols, Solemn Dreams.* Times Books, 1983.

7. Smith, Hedrick. *The Russians.* Times Books, 1983.

8. Sullivan, George. *Mikhail Gorbachev.* Julian Messner, 1988.

ABOUT THE AUTHOR

Steven Otfinoski has published many young adult novels, nonfiction books, and classroom plays. He lives in Stratford, Connecticut with his wife and two children.